Praise for
I Am an Adult Who Grew Up in an Alcoholic Family

"Tom Perrin speaks to us all from a wealth of experience and wisdom gained in his years of commitment to the Adult Child Movement. His observations are validating and insightful, offering something for everyone."

> —Ann Smith, Executive Director, Caron Family Services, The Caron Foundation, and author of *Grandchildren of Alcoholics*

"Tom Perrin has written a practical book that will be an important addition to personal and professional collections. It offers a unique view of addiction that will be an effective tool in both personal recovery and professional understanding."

> —Caroline V. Bridges, C.S.W., A.C.S.W.

"The chapter containing the 14 criteria to determine whether a therapist or program is good or bad is alone worth the price of the book! The account of his first AA meeting is an eye-opener that may well jolt some readers into identifying their own unrecognized dependence on alcohol. Likewise, his discussion of spirituality and God is remarkable in its very simplicity and winnowing away of trappings. The book's scholarship is enormous but not ostentatious. An amazingly useful book!"

> —Maxwell N. Weisman, M.D.

"In this engaging book, Tom Perrin writes less about his personal history than about the process of recovery, both as an alcoholic and, most importantly, as an adult from an alcoholic family. As such, it can be helpful to thousands of other recovering 'adult children.'"

> —Sheila B. Blume, M.D., Medical Director, Alcoholism, Chemical Dependency, and Compulsive Gambling Programs, South Oaks Hospital, Amityville, New York

"Combining personal experience with a wide range of source material, Tom Perrin issues a pleasant challenge to think and to reflect, one that can be enjoyed by the casual reader as well as interested readers. A delightful tour de force!"

> —Paul Curtin, founder and Director of Alcohol Services, Inc., Syracuse, New York, and author of *Tumbleweeds: A Therapist's Guide to Treatment of ACOAs*

"Wonderful and enlightening. Not only does the book connect many difficult issues such as codependence, the 'disease concept of chemical dependence,' adult children, sex addiction, and overeating, it also gives specific and poignant examples from Tom's life which touched me deeply. As a physician in the field of dependency, and personally recovering myself, I found this book to be a great teacher."

> —John Lichtenstein, M.D.

"An original and engaging account, full of wisdom. Tom Perrin's words not only make us think, they warm the heart as they describe the journey of recovery and the healing powers of family love and devotion."

> —Emily J. Marlin, psychotherapist and author of *Genograms* and *Relationships in Recovery*

"Tom Perrin, a bookseller turned book creator, makes you want to start a lively conversation or correspondence with him. Passionately involved yet objective, his frankness inspires others to be honest also, most importantly with themselves."

> —James E. Royce, Professor of Addiction Studies, Seattle University, and author of *Alcohol Problems and Alcoholism*

"Courageous and insightful. . .Tom Perrin has reached into all corners of research in this newly formed field. His book is a valuable tool for professionals who work in the field and is of tremendous assistance to individuals who are struggling with the consequences of their parents' alcoholism. We recommend it and are positive that it will become a significant reference."

> —Riley W. Regan, M.S.W., Executive Director, Governor's Council on Alcoholism and Drug Abuse, State of New Jersey

I Am an Adult Who Grew Up in an Alcoholic Family

Thomas W. Perrin

CONTINUUM • NEW YORK

1991
The Continuum Publishing Company
370 Lexington Avenue
New York, NY 10017

Printed in the United States of America

Library of Congress Cataloging-in-Publication Data

Perrin, Thomas W. (Thomas William), 1942–
    I am an adult who grew up in an alcoholic family / Thomas W.
Perrin.
        p.   cm.
    ISBN 0-8264-0498-7
    1. Adult children of alcoholics—Psychology.   2. Adult children of
alcoholics—Mental Health.   3. Alcoholism—Diagnosis.   I. Title.
    HV5132.P495   1991
    362.29'23—dc20   90-49436
                                                              CIP

This book is dedicated to Janice and Charlie with love, affection, and hope.

Contents

1 ......

I Am an Adult Who Grew Up in an Alcoholic Family

Once I thought I was unique, different, and alone. Certainly the disease of alcoholism kept me ignorant and isolated. The disease told me not to wash my family's linen in public. I obeyed, and so suffered in silence. I survived the disease of my parents only to acquire it myself.

Knowing only that I was affected by alcoholism, I began my recovery, sometimes in Al-Anon, sometimes in Alcoholics Anonymous. For a long time, there was this nagging awareness that once I had dealt with the problem of the moment, I would have to deal with the alcoholism of my family of origin, and its effects on my character. In spite of the progress I had made in my recovery, I was still getting in trouble, still having difficulty with other people. Peace of mind seemed to last only until I created the next crisis.

Some of the answers were sought in therapy. Sometimes I was told that I was sick, sometimes that I was just wrong. Mostly I was told that the answers were to be found within myself. I insisted that I did not know the answers. I wasn't even sure how to ask the questions. It never occurred to "them" that I might be truly ignorant rather than neurotic or crazy.

Then I began to discover other Adult Children of Alcoholics. Slowly at first, we shared our experiences, feelings, and behaviors. I discovered in ourselves a common history, despite having been raised generations and miles apart. I was no longer alone!

As my trust began to build, the walls came down, if only for a short time. I learned again to feel the hurt and cry where before I could not. Some of my behavior patterns had turned into habits and were causing me difficulty in my job and in my family life. I came to understand that my past and my present formed a pattern. Once I had identified my feelings and my behaviors, I began to understand myself better. I resolved to change myself whenever I could, knowing that it would not be easy to alter the habits of a lifetime.

Here are some of the things I found out about myself and that I am now beginning to change.

1. I guess at what normal is.
2. I have difficulty following projects through from beginning to end.
3. I lie when it would be just as easy to tell the truth.
4. I judge myself without mercy.
5. I have difficulty having fun.
6. I take myself very seriously.
7. I have difficulty with intimate relationships.
8. I overreact to changes over which I have no control.
9. I feel different from other people.
10. I constantly seek approval and affirmation.
11. I am super responsible or super irresponsible.
12. I am extremely loyal even in the face of evidence that the loyalty is undeserved.
13. I look for immediate as opposed to deferred gratification.
14. I lock myself into a course of action without giving serious consideration to alternate behaviors or possible consequences.
15. I seek tension and crisis and then complain about the results.
16. I avoid conflict or aggravate it; rarely do I deal with it.
17. I fear rejection and abandonment, yet I am rejecting of others.
18. I fear failure, but sabotage my success.
19. I fear criticism and judgment, yet I criticize and judge others.
20. I manage my time poorly and do not set my priorities in a way that works well for me.

In order to change, I cannot use my history as an excuse for continuing my behaviors. I have no regrets for what might have been, for my experiences have shaped my talents as well as my defects of character. It is my responsibility to discover these talents, to build my self esteem and to repair any damage done. I will allow myself to feel my feelings, to accept them, and learn to express them appropriately. When I have begun these tasks, I will try to let go of my past and get on with the business of managing my life.

I have survived against impossible odds until today. With the help of God and my friends, I shall survive the next twenty-four hours. I am no longer alone.

What I have learned about myself is of little value unless it is shared with others. I must confess, however, that before writing this book I had considerable doubt as to whether another book about adult children of alcoholics was really needed. Hasn't the subject been hashed to death? Hasn't the whole idea of adult children of alcoholics been superseded by evolving concepts of codependency? Who cares, anyway?

The ultimate justification for this book is whether or not it helps you, the reader, in some small way. Does it reach right down inside you and help heal a hurt that has long been hidden, hidden so deep you forgot that hurt existed? Does this book provide answers to lifelong questions you didn't know you needed to ask? Does it validate solutions that you had already guessed at?

Life is an ancient mosaic, a jigsaw puzzle of wonderful complexity and infinite interest. The meaning to some of the parts of life I have found for myself I share here. I have described enough of a pattern or outline that you will begin to fill in for yourself those pieces of the puzzle uniquely yours or held in common with others close to you. My picture does not have to be your picture. Yet, if your experience in some way resembles my experience, then that is a pattern you might want to pay some attention to. If part or all of this pattern is shared by still another person, then that may provide a strong motivation to fill in as many of the adjoining pieces of the puzzle as you can. In any event, it's an extraordinarily interesting journey. I wish you well.

If what I have written does any of these things, then this will be a needed and useful book, regardless of the quantity and quality of other books on the same subjects.

I have much more selfish reasons for writing, however. I've waited a long time to finish this book. Too long a time. To paraphrase Joseph Conrad, there is no rest for the messenger until the message is delivered. Parts of this message were formulated in my mind shortly after I stopped drinking in 1975. Other parts have evolved over the years and represent much more recent developments in my thought and experience. These ideas, put into practice over the last fifteen years, need to be tested in the marketplace of thought. I need to know if my ideas work on a grander scale than that of my own intimate circle of friends, clients, and acquaintances.

Everything in this book is theoretical. That means none of what is written here is true until tested by you. I've limited my discussions and essays to areas that have worked well for myself, over time. Thus, what is written here is practical as well as theoretical. But because my sample of one is so small, you should be cautious until you have demonstrated that what is written here works for you as well. If all that happens is that I've made you think, and that as a result of that thought you have found a different solution or explanation from the one presented here, then I will be content.

2 ...

Characteristics of the Adult Child

All my life, I felt that I was laboring under some kind of dark cloud that followed me wherever I went, preventing me from being in the right place at the right time, from knowing what was going on, from knowing what to do in any situation. I was always too late or too early. I could never get it right. I either put my foot in my mouth or tripped over it. I had never heard of self-confidence or self-esteem. I had never had either of them. I was always held back and when I was pushed up front by some fluke, I never knew what to do next. I had great and wonderful ideas. Somehow I never got to see these wonderful ideas come to life and become part of my reality. I was a failure full of unrealized potential, which unnerved me and confused my associates. I wanted to be a good person. I tried to be a good person, but my noble efforts always ended buried in a dunghill. I was a rough diamond, abrasive on the outside with the precious inside hidden where only I knew where to find it.

It was to take me many years before I would find out that my many discomforts could be traced to my alcoholic family environment and many more to discover that others could be traced to a genetic background.

In order to survive our childhood, we acquire a number of characteristics to survive. Now that we've grown up, these characteristics are no longer necessary. Instead, they are increasingly uncomfortable.

My list of characteristics of Adult Children of Alcoholics had its origin in a small group of men and women, myself among them, who met in the living room of Dr. Janet Woititz in the late winter and spring of 1981. Dr. Woititz drew on some of her experience in that group to write her best-selling book, *Adult Children of Alcoholics*.[1] In December 1981, I wrote the characteristics in their present form for use by a self-help group. Ultimately, they became part of a brochure promoting my workshops for adult children of alcoholics. As a result of the experience gained in those workshops, I expanded the original thirteen characteristics to twenty.

Characteristics of adult children of alcoholics have their own characteristics. For example, many of them are bipolar. That is, a person may exhibit either or both of an extreme of a particular behavior. This makes these characteristics very difficult to quantify or to test properly. None of the characteristics are directly due to alcohol use or misuse by a parent. At one time, I believed their origin probably lay more in the emotional abuse and neglect of children than from any other cause. I suspected this was true because grandchildren of alcoholics with teetotaling parents tend to identify strongly with these statements. I have recently discovered[2] that many of these characteristics are symptoms of Attention Deficit Disorder (ADD) and Attention Deficit Disorder with Hyperactivity (ADHD), which have long been known to be associated with children of alcoholics. The genetic linkage of ADD/ADHD falls into the same model that I propose for alcoholism. I am, therefore, no longer willing to attribute all of these characteristics to parental misconduct.

I won't presume to tell you that all adult children of alcoholic parents have all of these characteristics.[3] They are simply behaviors or thought patterns that I have or have had. They have been a

1. Woititz, J.G. (1983). *Adult children of alcoholics*. Deerfield Beach, FL: Health Communications.

2. Comings, David E. (1990). *Tourette syndrome and human behavior*. Duarte, CA: Hope Press. and American Psychiatric Association. (1987). *Diagnostic and statistical manual of mental disorders*. 3rd Ed. rev). Washington DC: Author.

3. Further discussions of these characteristics can be read in Ackerman, R. (1987). *Let go and grow*. Deerfield Beach, FL: Health Communications. and in Ackerman, R. (1987) *Same house, different homes*. Deerfield Beach, FL: Health Communications.

source of aggravation and annoyance for most of my life. This is a clear case in which recovery comes in two parts: the first is in describing the symptom, the second in finding out how to extinguish the behavior. After reading how I interpret each characteristic, you may or may not identify with the behavior. If you do identify with the behavior, your life may be made much easier by changing the behavior. Depending on your individual psychological and genetic makeup, some characteristics may be easier to extinguish than others. Some of the more resistant ones, especially those of possible genetic origin, may take the better part of a lifetime to overcome.

I Guess at What Normal Is

The operative word here is *guess*. To guess at whatever exists is to distort the reality checking process.

When I was a young child, I would ask questions of my adults. I was told, in reply: (a) don't bother the adult, (b) the question was of no importance, (c) the answer was of no use to me, (d) don't ask questions, (e) do as I was told; or I was given an answer to a question other than the one I asked. All of these messages are frustratingly painful and productive of low self-esteem.

What I learned from my adults was not to ask questions. I was to do as I was told. I was to keep quiet. I was to stay out of the way. I was not to question authority. But what's a kid to do if he wants to understand how his universe works?

What I did was to learn from clues, small pieces of information randomly acquired and systematically sorted in my mind. I drew conclusions from small bits of information. I read books. God, did I read! I read *The Book of Knowledge*, the *Columbia Encyclopedia*, and every book that my family had acquired over three generations. I learned to read minds. I became very intuitive. I became an information junkie, believing that knowledge was power. My military service was spent in an intelligence unit where my intuitive skills were given structure and reinforced.

But I never learned to ask questions in a way that would elicit answers. As a child, my mother would tease me, saying that my response to anything was "Iknowit." No one could tell me anything. I already knew the answers.

The problem was that I was *not* right all the time. In spite of my considerable skills, I was probably wrong a good twenty percent of the time. Now, an eighty percent success rate is not to be dismissed lightly. However, a twenty percent failure rate was enough to get me in trouble with just about anybody who counted. Nobody likes a know-it-all, much less someone who needs to be right all the time. I was well into my recovery when I discovered that my habitual failure to ask directions when I was lost could be considered arrogance.

My friends didn't like the idea of having their minds read. They felt insulted. They felt misunderstood. I couldn't understand why they felt that way since I could read their minds.

There's no fun in guessing all the time. It makes me feel insecure and leads to feelings of being disconnected from the rest of the universe.

It was suggested to me that whenever I felt I knew the answer, especially when I was mind reading, to check it out, to make inquiries, to ask questions, to get confirmation of what I was thinking. I resisted the idea. Not only was I sure that I was always right, but if I wasn't I didn't want to know. And then there was that emotional logic that said if I asked questions, someone might think me ignorant. To be ignorant was to be inadequate. To be inadequate was to be a nothing, the lowest of the low. That was unacceptable, so I didn't ask questions.

When noise and chaos in the home are chronic, everyday happenings, it is difficult to imagine what serenity might be like. Similarly, when the abuse of a person is chronic, it becomes difficult to imagine what the total absence of abuse might be like.

What's upside down becomes right side up. What is abnormal becomes normal. What was once—or should have been—normal becomes forgotten. Normal doesn't mean "healthy" or "right." It's just a word to describe something that happens a lot. When something happens so often that it's normal, it's also "normal" to justify its existence simply because "everybody does it." As you can see, it's easy to get confused.

What's normal about child abuse? First, it happens a lot. Child abuse happens so much and so often that what it is gets lost in all the other everyday activities. It loses its meaning. Many children of alcoholics will deny that they were ever abused by their parent. As children, they could not reconcile the treatment they received from their parents with the love they expected. In order to deal with this incongruity, many children of alcoholics invented the myth that they "deserved" the treatment they received. They were "bad," they said. Never mind that their parents' actions were wholly out of proportion to their behavior. It is not surprising that many children of alcoholics grow into adulthood still thinking that they were bad.

What is child abuse? In the alcoholic family, the most common form of abuse is emotional abuse. Few, if any, children of alcoholics escape it. It often consists of scapegoating the child, not providing a loving environment, threatening, corrupting, terrorizing, or rejecting the child. Children in such an environment cannot, except with great difficulty, thrive and grow emotionally.

When discipline produces injury that requires medical treatment, that is child abuse. Note that a minor child is not competent to refuse medical treatment. Hitting with a closed fist, a belt, lamp cord, or kicking, inflicting burns, or throwing a child all constitute child abuse.

Physical neglect of the child in the alcoholic family is often present where the mother is the single parent and also the alcoholic. Where drugs other than alcohol are also abused, the likelihood of physical neglect is markedly increased. Neglect means failure to provide such everyday necessities as nourishing food, appropriate clothing, supervision, shelter, or medical treatment, even when the family has the financial means to do so.

Child sexual abuse is any activity whereby the child or adolescent is *used* to gratify the sexual needs or desires of an adult or older sibling. It is commonly thought that child sexual abuse is limited to sexual intercourse. However, sexual abuse toward minor children of either sex is comprised of a wide range of behavior by parents, parent figures, and caretakers. These include provocative nudity and disrobing, genital exposure, peeping, kissing in ways reserved for adults, fondling, masturbation, fellatio, cunnilingus, penetration of the anus or vagina by a finger or by any foreign object, dry intercourse, and lastly, intercourse.[4] All of these behaviors are commonly perpetrated upon children and adolescents by adults. None

---

4. Sgroi, S.M. (1982). *Handbook of clinical intervention in child sexual abuse.* Lexington, MA: Lexington Books.

of these behaviors are caused by the victims. None of these behaviors are beneficial.

While we're discussing child sexual abuse, I will note that men
are victims and survivors almost as often as women. The catch is,
we don't talk about it, even among ourselves. It is among our
deepest and darkest secrets, whether the perpetrator is a parent,
parent figure, or therapist.[5]

I Have Difficulty Following Projects Through from Beginning to End

This one hurts to write about, because it is one that remains
difficult a decade after I first wrote it down. Part of my difficulty lies
in that I had no model for finishing projects. Let me illustrate.

Some years ago, I was taking a spring drive on a back road in
New York's North Country. Off to the right I noticed that someone had begun to tear down an old farmhouse. In the fall of the
same year, I noticed that the house demolition had been completed,
a cap put on the cellar, all the demolition debris had been removed,
and new grass sown in the yard. The following year, a new house
was built on the old foundation, and the new establishment is as
clean as a suburban development. What's extraordinary about this
little tale is that I don't know how to do that. My father's house in
the same neighborhood was begun in 1952. Almost thirty years
later, there is still the remains of the original construction debris
lying about. I rarely, if ever, saw anyone in my family finish anything. Getting through college was not a test of intelligence, but
rather a test of endurance. I would quit every semester around
midterm examinations, and then decide to grind it out.

There is an emotional logic to procrastination. I can't be judged
on unfinished product; therefore, I don't finish it. In recovery, I
have learned that it takes much more energy to finish something
that is unfinished. My solution has been to delegate some projects,
either to employees or to professionals. My income taxes are now

---

5. There are now a number of publications for men who were sexually abused
by adults. The best of these are Hunter, M. (1990). *Abused boys.* Lexington, MA:
Lexington Books; Lew, M. (1990). *Victims no longer.* New York: HarperCollins.

done on time, but only because I am willing to pay professionals to do them for me. I have learned that there is no shame in hiring people to do what I am capable of doing, but don't want to do. For employers who are themselves children of alcoholics and who employ children of alcoholics, this can be a complex and frustrating characteristic. To deal with it, I have learned, painfully, that successful delegation means supervision and follow-up. For the adult child as employer, this means finishing the project.

Every adult child I ever met works best under pressure. Not finishing things is a characteristic of Attention Deficit Disorder. One of the ways we have evolved to cope with this characteristic is to let the pressure build up until we have enough momentum to carry something through to its final conclusion. Although this is dysfunctional, I see it as a tribute to our unconscious ability to deal with a disorder we didn't know we had.

Finishing things does not mean perfection. It means cleaning out *all* of a closet, not leaving the top shelf a mess. For computer programmers, it means fully documenting your work. For dishwashers, it means washing all the dirty dishes, and not leaving a dirty glass on the kitchen table. I swear I spend more energy on the things I have left behind than on the whole of what went before. Sometimes, I just have to grind it out and stay on the job until the job is done.

When I was an undergraduate, I was fortunate enough to study under a very wise professor of medieval history, Walter Wakefield. I'm sure Dr. Wakefield hated to come to work when I was in his class, because I always gave him a hard time. Nevertheless, he taught me how to narrow a subject down to manageable proportions. All I had to do, he said, was to define exactly what it was I wanted to do, and then to do it. If my project was too big, and I didn't finish it, I would fail the course. No matter how small I defined my project, if I finished what I said I would do, I would pass. I handed in the shortest paper in the class, but it was very carefully crafted. Of all the courses I took from Wakefield, my A in Medieval History was one of my proudest achievements.

To finish some things, whether it's this book or any other project, sometimes means just grinding it out. One way to fool the emotional logic of this characteristic is to divide a project into smaller pieces. These smaller projects in time add up to a significant body of work. The computer has turned out to be a wonderful tool for chronic procrastinators, because it has made perfection possible. Where before I would refuse to revise and edit a laboriously type-written manuscript, the computer now makes revision and editing a creative journey instead of a painful chore. The danger here is that eventually, one must let go of one's magnum opus, and let it see the light of day.

It's important for the adult child to understand that he or she is the only one who can approve a work. If the public likes it, that's icing on the cake. If they don't, that's too bad. It is enough that we do. We must learn to be competent judges of our own work.

I Lie When It Would Be Just as Easy to Tell the Truth

I suspect that most children of alcoholics are painfully honest. Yet, most of us end up being defensive at one time or another. When we're being confronted, or even *think* we're being con-fronted, it's very difficult to pin us down. We're evasive. We want to know *why* you want to know what you're asking before we'll give you a straight answer. We want assurance that the answer will not harm us.

When I was a young person, I became a very accomplished liar. Whenever my father asked me something, my answers were invari-ably criticized or cross examined. I eventually learned to stop giving straight answers. If my answer was criticized, I could then discard the criticism as being of no practical value because what I gave him wasn't true anyway.

At other times, I would elaborate upon the truth, and make things grander than they were in order to receive recognition or attention.

Later, I was to find that it was easier to tell the truth about things, and evade the truth about my feelings. When I evaded the truth by being defensive, my therapist would ask me what it was that I was defending. The answer was always a feeling rooted in my past. Once I was able to accept my feelings and deal with them, I discovered that truth was the ultimate weapon. If you didn't like the truth, that was too bad. Because I knew myself better than anyone, I could not be destroyed by the truth.

I find it very difficult to watch situation comedies on television. Many of them would have no story line if their characters didn't lie when it was just as easy to tell the truth. But their writers perpetuate the idea that telling the truth is awful, and that telling lies is funny.

Personally, I'm a little sick and tired of cover-ups, especially at the government level. It's time we learned to ask ourselves, "What's the worst that could happen if I told the truth?"[6]

I Judge Myself Without Mercy

I once read that at the Last Judgment we would judge ourselves. I thought, how cruel, for surely we would all consign ourselves to Hell. No judge could be harsher and more unfair than ourselves. Never are we poorer judges of character than when we judge ourselves. We hold ourselves in very low esteem. We do not think we are worthy—of a good job, a bank loan, a college education, or a wonderful spouse. So we settle for second best or none at all.

Should a stray compliment float by, we reject it out of hand. Surely the compliment belongs to someone else, certainly not to me. (And if that compliment is paid to someone else, we nurse a resentment for weeks.) We judge ourselves so hard we won't accept criticism from others. We just can't stand a little more negative information about us.

Many of us have a great deal of difficulty with the Fourth Step of Alcoholics Anonymous, which states that we "made a fearless and searching moral inventory of ourselves." Personally, I've always had trouble with the fearless part. I never did a Fourth Step yet without a considerable amount of apprehension over what I would find. After all, who enjoys looking at oneself, especially when there's so much garbage lying about? When I first encountered this Step, I thought it meant that I had to catalog every sin of omission and commission. Indeed, in the early days of AA, that's just what it meant. This Step, as originally written in 1938, said, "We made a moral inventory of our defects or sins."[7]

With this in mind, it was a great comfort to read Abraham Maslow, who wrote that our inner nature is good or neutral rather

---

6. The answer, of course, is that the truth will set you free, but first it will piss you off.

7. Pittman, B. (1988). *AA the way it began*. Seattle: Glen Abbey Books.

than bad. Our defects are not intrinsic, but rather seem to be violent reactions against the frustration of our intrinsic needs, emotions, and capacities.[8] I interpreted this to mean that whatever the behaviors I had acquired during the course of my life, I was fundamentally good at the core of my being, or at worst, neutral. With this reassurance, I could embark on a searching, if not fearless, inventory of myself.

More recently, Matthew Fox has rejected the idea of original sin. The concept that our fundamental character is sinfully tainted has no basis in scripture. Rather, he says, "we burst into the world as 'original blessings.'"[9]

Most of us know what we're doing wrong. It's not a great secret, either to ourselves or to others. But do we know what we're doing right? Not by a long shot. When it was suggested that for my Fourth Step inventory to be done properly I had to list my character assets, gifts, and talents as well as my defects, I was at a loss as to where to begin. It was further suggested, that in order not to be morally bankrupt, my books had to balance, my credits needed to equal my debits. So I had to scramble, either to reduce my bad habits or to acquire new, good ones.

I Have Difficulty Having Fun

Nothing strikes fear deeper into my heart than the prospect of having fun. What other people do for fun makes me break out into a nervous sweat. Games and dancing imply the need to perform, or the possible exposure to ridicule. Uncomfortableness of the worst kind accompanies fun. I do not seek it.

When asked, "What do you do for fun?" I hem and haw, stumble and mumble. I have no clear answer. What the hell is fun, anyway?

My primary pleasures are solitary. I work, I read, I drive on long trips. I meditate and I think. I listen to music and watch the tube. That is what I do for fun. And usually, I do two or more of the above at a time. The thought of having empty time leaves me anxious and restless.

8. Maslow, A.H. (1962). *Toward a psychology of being.* (2nd Ed.) New York: Van Nostrand.

9. Fox, M. (1983). *Original blessing.* Santa Fe, NM: Bear & Company.

When I was a teenager, before I discovered alcohol, I had time for different kinds of fun. In those days, I couldn't get a job. There were no jobs for teenagers. So I played, and played well. Ask me to play now, and I feel guilty. As much as I need and want a vacation each year, I have to force myself to plan my weeks away from home. Never mind that the stress of my daily life needs a break, the thought of taking a vacation brings with it its own stress. I don't begin to relax until the beginning of the second week of vacation, and who can afford a second week away from the job?

If I am successful in having one kind of fun, that does not necessarily mean that I will be successful at another kind. I have difficulty generalizing from one kind of fun to another. That means that I have to work through the same old feelings all over again each time a new kind of fun comes along. In order to have real fun I need to let go of the guilt that gets in the way. For this I seem to need permission. One measure of my success in dealing with this characteristic is *my* ability to give *me* permission to have fun, rather than waiting for permission to come from others.

I was once the beneficiary of an all-expense-paid week in Nantucket, courtesy of a very dear and beloved friend. As I was sitting in the plane waiting to taxi down the runway, I had this fleeting thought that if the plane crashed, I wouldn't have to take a week off, and I could go back to work. I think it's interesting that my friends have to engineer me into a situation where I find it difficult to refuse to have fun. I often have to be dragged kicking and screaming into a situation where I will feel good. There is a part of me that would rather sit on the outside being miserable watching people on the inside having a good time, wanting to be right in there with them, but fearing rejection and ridicule. The torture is really unnecessary. Healthy people naturally want outsiders to share in their feelings of fun. The only cure is to say the hell with it and jump in. The worst that could happen is for me to reject myself.

I often wonder whether or not my difficulty with this characteristic comes from my role in my family, the scapegoat. Heroes, and Lost Children may feel as I do, but perhaps the Mascot/Clown experiences fun in a different light.

Some of my healthier friends, under the guise of entertaining their children, have invited us to amusement parks. I, as the wise but corpulent uncle, have tagged along, but only to watch the children. Much to my surprise, I have found myself having fun at the games, my favorite being the water slides. Having fun is far too important to be left to children. Another sort of fun for adults are the new games, first popularized by Andrew Fluegelman.[10] Fluegelman was the creative genius who came up with games where my serious side could have fun without the risk of losing. I could play hard, think hard, and not get hurt emotionally in the process. I could also work on my touch issues without having to think or worry about sexual involvement.

I Take Myself Very Seriously

This characteristic, taking oneself very seriously, is often associated with difficulty in having fun, but for me the two characteristics are quite different. For most of my life, life appeared grim. It seemed I was always struggling for survival. What I thought important didn't seem to be as important to others. Life remains a serious business. I insist on being taken seriously. Don't tease me. Don't pull my leg. I can't stand being ridiculed. It's not that I have no sense of humor. I just can't remember a joke or a punch line. What's worse, I often fail to recognize that other people have a sense of humor.

It took me a long time to figure out that my son Charlie had a sense of humor—that he wasn't being difficult—but was just playing tricks on me. When he was a couple of years old, Charlie tossed a soccer ball under the car. While I was reaching under the car to

---

10. See Fluegelman, A. (1976). *New games*. New York: Doubleday. Fluegelman was an extraordinary man who apparently had no control issues. Among his other accomplishments, he introduced the concept of free computer software (Freeware). If you liked the software after having tried it, you could send in a donation and get the documentation. More recently, Paul O., whose story is published in *Alcoholics Anonymous,* published a working guide to the Twelve Steps. *(An unofficial guide to the twelve steps.)* If the book worked for you, you sent in a donation to cover the printing costs. Other new games books include Fluegelman, A. (1981). *More new games*. New York: Doubleday; Weinstein, M. & Goodman, J. (1980). *Playfair*. San Luis Obispo, CA: Impact; Moe, J. & Pohlman, D. (1989). *Kids power healing games for children of alcoholics*. Deerfield Beach, FL: Health Communications; LeFevre, D.N. (1988). *New games for the whole family*. New York: Putnam; and Orlick, T. (1975). *Cooperative sports and games book*. New York: Pantheon.

secure the ball, Charlie disappeared, all in the space of microseconds. After much panic yelling and running around the schoolyard, I found him a hundred yards away, eyes shut and leaning against a telephone pole, playing hide and seek. And I was "it." He was joking and laughing, and I was terror-stricken. What I learned that day was that Charlie had a sense of humor. He liked to fool his dad. When I was able to interpret his behavior correctly, I panicked a lot less and was able to divert his joking behavior into less scary situations.

I Have Difficulty With Intimate Relationships

I'm sure that hundreds, if not thousands of volumes have been written on intimacy. Together with control issues, intimacy issues form the cornerstones of co-dependency. Name an intimacy issue and I have it.

I have found out a few things about intimacy. I crave it. I run away from it. When I get it, I am angry that I didn't get it before. Intimacy is scary. Intimacy is based on trust. Intimacy is not sex. Intimacy is not touching. Intimacy is not love. Intimacy is all of these things. Intimacy is warm, distance is cold. Intimacy is hard work. Intimacy is relief.

Above all, intimacy is complicated. All of our past and all of our partner's past combine into a very difficult present. It doesn't help that we often choose partners who have the same intimacy issues we do.

Children of alcoholics have a tendency to confuse sex, intimacy, love, and touching. They're all rolled up in the same ball, and it's a toss-up as to which one bounces first. To touch, even accidentally, implies a sexual relationship, or the fear of one. Sex is traded for intimacy, and thought, at first, to be an even exchange. Until we're taught otherwise, the only time we touch our partners is when we want sex.

I was never touched enough as a kid, and when I was, more often than not, it was violent. Small wonder that when it came to courtship, I was a little confused as to how to get close. It doesn't have to be that way. Now it's different. I've learned that touch doesn't have to be sexual. When I first started running workshops for adult children of alcoholics, I devoted an entire period to a touching exercise. This period evoked more anxiety than any other feature of the workshop. Given the tension, one would think I had scheduled a nude encounter group. Here is the exercise, in its entirety.

At some time of your own choosing during the next week, I want you to hold hands with another person of your choice. It can be while you are saying the closing prayer at a meeting. It can be while you are walking down the street with your partner. It can be with a stranger, it can be with your child or spouse. Just hold hands. And while you are holding hands, I want you to concentrate on the feeling of your skin against the skin of another person. While you are concentrating on this feeling, I want you to continue to hold on to that person's hand, even if you feel like tearing it away. I want you to feel the feeling of skin against skin in all its dimensions. And then I want you to come back to group next week and share with the group what you experienced and what it was like for you.

This is a very difficult exercise. For the sexually abused, it is a first step toward regaining our sensuality. For all of us who were abused, either physically, emotionally, or sexually, it is a critical part of our recovery to learn how to touch and be touched in a safe way. I think most of us are skin hungry. We do not now, and never did, get enough safe touching. Yet, we need to feel skin, and we need to feel it in safe, nonsexual, nonexploitative ways.

One of the more extraordinary sensate focus exercises we can teach ourselves and our children is to close our eyes, and feel/ explore the face of another person with our fingers. I have seen adults misinterpret this exercise as sexual and be frightened by it. But if we are to regain access to our feelings, it is very helpful. Another safe therapy is the hug. I personally love hugs, but I'm always grateful to the person who asks permission first, and I always ask before giving one. Given our history of sexual exploitation and physical/emotional abuse, we need to respect our own pain and that of others, and not intrude upon boundaries without permission.

I Overreact to Changes Over Which I Have No Control

There are two central issues that unite adult children of alcoholics and other codependents: *control* and *intimacy*. I have little good to say about control issues, which may be why I overreact to them. For that matter, I don't like change that much either.

Quite a few years ago, Dr. Thomas H. Holmes of the University of Washington School of Medicine did some original research in which he found that changes in major life events were stressful. The stress induced by such changes had adverse effects on the health of those persons experiencing the stress. When the score equals 150 or more for twelve months, there is an increased chance of getting sick. Scores of 300 or more on this scale place a person in a major life crisis. Rita and Blair Justice took Dr. Holmes's Schedule of Recent Life Experience (see table) one step further, and found that excessive change was often a contributory factor in child abuse. As they pointed out, different people react differently to stress. One has a heart attack, another gets depressed, and still another may beat his kid or commit incest.[11]

When I first came across this schedule, I was amazed at how many matches there are between these life events and the natural history of alcoholic and ACOA families. Alcoholics and their families attempt geographic cures,[12] get divorced, experience illness, and change their financial state almost as often as they change their clothes. Their recovery is as stressful as their illness, if not more so. When I gave this schedule to adult children of alcoholics, their average score was between 200 and 300 points. Those who were in on-again, off-again (cling-clung, highly co-dependent) relationships had scores as high as 6,000. Little wonder they got sick a lot.

What the Justices pointed out was that much of this change is manageable. I now monitor this schedule every three to six months. If the score is too high, I know that it is not the time to get a new job or leave an old one. If I have just bought a house, it may be wiser (that is, less stressful) to wait a while before making major

---

11. Justice, B. & Justice, R. (1979). *The broken taboo*. New York: Human Sciences Press.

12. I apologize for the jargon. A geographic cure is the notion that one's problems of the moment will be cured if one moves to a different location, changes job or career, dumps a lover, etc. The catch is that *we* are the problem, and we follow ourselves everywhere. The cure is to "blossom where you are."

Schedule of Recent Life Experience
after Thomas H. Holmes, MD (1978)
(Record Number of Changes Occuring within the Past Twelve Months

1. Under "Number of Occurences" indicate how many times in the past twelve months each of the events has occurred
2. Multiply the number under "Scale Value" by the number of occurrences of each event and place the answer under "Your Score."
3. Add the figures under "Your Score" to find your total for the past year.

	Number of occurrences	Scale Value	Your Score
Health			
Major personal injury or illness (hospitalization for week or more)	_____	53	_____
Major change in eating habits (a lot more or a lot less food intake, or very different meal hours or surroundings)	_____	15	_____
Major change in sleeping habits (a lot more or a lot less sleep, or change in part of a day when asleep)	_____	17	_____
Major change in usual type and/or amount of recreation.	_____	19	_____
Work			
Retirement from work	_____	45	_____
Major change in responsibilities at work (e.g. promotion, demotion, lateral transfer)	_____	29	_____
Being fired or laid off from work	_____	47	_____
Changing to different line of work	_____	36	_____
Troubles with the boss	_____	23	_____
Major business readjustment (merger, bankruptcy, reorganization)	_____	39	_____
Major change in working hours or conditions	_____	20	_____

	Number of occurrences	Scale Value	Your Score
Home and Family			
Death of a spouse	_____	100	_____
Marital separation from mate	_____	65	_____
Divorce	_____	73	_____
Marriage	_____	50	_____
Marital reconciliation with mate	_____	45	_____
Death of a close family member	_____	63	_____
Pregnancy	_____	40	_____
Gaining a new family member (birth, adoption, moving in, etc)	_____	39	_____
In-law troubles	_____	29	_____
Spouse beginning or ceasing to work outside home	_____	26	_____
Son or daughter leaving home (marriage, college)	_____	29	_____
Major change in number of family get-togethers (e.g. a lot more or a lot less than usual)	_____	15	_____
Major change in the number of arguments with spouse (e.g. a lot more or a lot less than usual)	_____	35	_____
Financial			
Taking on a mortgage greater than $20,000 (e.g. purchasing a home or business)	_____	31	_____
Taking on a mortgage or loan less than $20,000. (e.g. car purchase)	_____	17	_____
Foreclosure on a mortgage or loan	_____	30	_____
Major change in financial state (e.g. a lot worse off or a lot better off than usual)	_____	38	_____

	Number of occurrences	Scale Value	Your Score
Personal and Social			
Sexual difficulties	————	39	————
Outstanding personal achievement	————	28	————
Major change in living conditions (building new home, remodeling, deterioration of building or neighborhood)	————	25	————
Change in residence	————	20	————
Changing to a new school	————	20	————
Revision of personal habits (dress, manners, associations	————	24	————
Vacation	————	13	————
Christmas	————	12	————
Minor violations of the law (speeding tickets, etc)	————	11	————
Detention in jail or other institution	————	63	————
Major change in church activities (a lot more or a lot less than usual)	————	19	————
Major change in social activities	————	18	————
This is your total life change for the last twelve months			————

alterations. I can do all that I want to do. I just need to stretch it out a bit, and let some time go by before making major life changes. At the moment, my score is 101, just enough to make life interesting. When I discovered the Holmes scale, my score reached 600 and more, and I was going crazy on a daily basis. I've found that just about every time my stress level gets too high, my body says it needs a break and gets sick. But since I now control my stress level, I just don't get sick anymore.[13]

---

13. The child who adopts the role of scapegoat in the family often gets physically sick or injured, far out of proportion to other siblings. The challenge for the adult child in recovery is to reverse this process by consciously staying well, and managing one's health consciously.

My way to deal with change was to control the change. I then had advance warning. I could mold the change to my own circumstances. Everybody else had to conform to my way of doing things. They suffered. I didn't. On the other hand, I surrounded myself with people who acted the way I did, so in the long run, nobody won.

I've since learned that it's better to telegraph change, to discuss proposed changes with others and to ask people for their input. I need to be less resistant, and less negative to changes put forward by others. I have to remind myself to ask, "How important is it?" before overreacting. (To be perfectly honest, I usually overreact first, and ask the question later, after I've worked it through a little.)

If you don't think that we have control issues, you might want to take a look at this paragraph from Melody Beattie's *Codependent No More*.

We nag; lecture; scream; holler; cry; beg; bribe, coerce, hover over; protect; accuse; chase after; run away from; try to talk into; try to talk out of; attempt to induce guilt in; seduce; entrap; check on; demonstrate how much we've been hurt; hurt people in return so they'll know how it feels; threaten to hurt ourselves; whip power plays on; deliver ultimatums to; do things for; refuse to do things for; stomp out on; get even with; whine; vent fury on; act helpless; suffer in loud silence; try to please; lie; do sneaky little things; do sneaky big things; clutch at our hearts and threaten to die; grab our heads and threaten to go crazy; beat on our chests and threaten to kill; enlist the aid of supporters; gauge our words carefully; sleep with; refuse to sleep with; have children with; bargain with; drag to counselling; drag out of counselling; talk mean about; talk mean to; insult; condemn; pray for miracles; pay for miracles; go to places we don't want to go; stay nearby; supervise; dictate; command; complain; write letters about; write letters to; stay home and wait for; go out and look for; call all over looking for; drive down dark alleys at night hoping to see; chase down dark alleys at night hoping to catch; run down dark alleys to get away from; bring home; keep home; lock out; move away from; move with; scold; impress upon; advise; teach lessons to; set straight; insist; give in to; placate; provoke; try to make jealous; try to make afraid; remind; inquire; hint; look through pockets; peek in wallets; search dresser drawers; dig through glove boxes; look in the toilet tank; try to look into the future; search through the past; call relatives about; reason with;

settle issues once and for all; settle them again; punish; reward; almost give up on; then try even harder.[14]

I believe that control issues are a life and death matter. Those who find the freedom inherent in giving up control are probably less likely to be obsessive, to have heart attacks, and to act impulsively. My own spiritual awakening had to do with giving up my need to control the outcome of events, even when I was right. The results were so startling in terms of personal freedom, that I continue to make my noncontrol of persons and things a personal issue on a daily basis. I ask myself, "What can *I* do about this (this minute, this day)?" When this question is asked in personal terms, and limited to the present, the range of options available to me becomes very clear. I then experience the freedom of directing my energies in appropriate and healthy directions. Sometimes the answers to my questions are not to my liking. The answers may be unpleasant, expensive, or costly in some emotional way. But because I have surrendered the issue, dealing with reality becomes a pleasure rather than a chore.

There is a flip side to this issue. Part of my program of recovery states that I will not be controlled (or manipulated, or used, or abused) by any person. This is one of my boundaries, and it is nonnegotiable.

I Feel Different from Other People

I've always perceived myself as different, apart from others. I never felt connected to other people, either individuals or groups. Whether the feeling was due to my isolation, my drinking, my alienation from the universe, or my genetic makeup, it didn't change when I got sober. And this was a great disappointment. Up until I got sober, I had dealt with this feeling by becoming a professional loner. I considered myself one of the elite, superior to others in ability and intelligence, but at the same time, secretly wanting to be one of them, whoever they were.

---

14. Beattie, M. *Codependent no more.* (1987). New York: Harper & Row. It can be argued that while not all co-dependents are adult children of alcoholics, all adult children of alcoholics are co-dependents.

I thought all this would change when I got sober. But my interests were different from those of my contemporaries in the self-help groups, and my commuter life-style inhibited getting friendly with my co-workers. My difficulties with intimacy inhibited me from forming new relationships, and so the vicious cycle continued unabated.

I sometimes wonder whether or not this feeling is rooted in our physiology. We are always looking for something to make us whole, but we don't know what is missing. Maybe we really are different from other people.

What changed to make this feeling disappear? Fifteen years after I stopped drinking, several themes emerge: I take better care of myself nutritionally. I take my vitamins daily and as a result, body and soul remain tightly integrated. I have a network of friends and acquaintances who know me and care for me. I am no longer isolated. I have a very select circle of soulmates with whom I can be emotionally intimate without risk of their betraying my trust and confidence. They know and protect my deepest and darkest secrets, and love me anyway. I have learned to be sensitive to the needs and feelings of others, as well as to my own needs and feelings. I no longer play the role of scapegoat, having abandoned it for more rewarding roles. I understand my loneliness and emptiness. I am connected to my universe.

I Constantly Seek Approval and Affirmation

My arrogance and elitism often got in the way of understanding this characteristic. I thought that I did not need anybody's approval. If self-will was ever to run riot, I could provide all the necessary. But I sure wanted the recognition, attention, approval, status—all that others would provide to fill my well of neediness. I wanted it, I craved it, I sold myself for it. It didn't have to be too public, a nod in my direction would do. I would not think of doing a project or a venture without partners, and when I could not get them, I abandoned the project. If I had an idea, I would share it looking for approval, and then be deflated when it didn't come. Of course, I always chose negativists from which to get approval, which is a little bit like trying to charcoal a steak using ice cubes for fuel.

The answer is that I am the only one who can satisfy my approval needs. When I'm creative, when I do a job, when I write, it is enough, it is sufficient, if I approve of it, if I like what I have accomplished. I get my jollies more from the perfection of my craft than from what my craft does for others. If others benefit from my work, that's wonderful for my Messiah complex. But my self-esteem is far too precious to allow others to tinker with it. To make my self-esteem dependent upon the approval of others is to invite others to control my emotional life.

When I first started running groups for adult children of alcoholics back in the early eighties, I was told that no one would come; that the traditional self-help groups provided for all the needs of adult children of alcoholics and that I was a bigot for teaching otherwise. I organized the groups because the groups themselves were sufficient reason for their existence. People did come and they stayed and recommended the groups to their friends. If that's bigotry, I'll wear it as a badge of honor. Had I waited for approval then, I might still be waiting.

There's some nice fringe benefits to this. When I practice this, I can't be manipulated or conned, I can't be bought, and I can't be sold down the river. When I do accomplish something, I can say that my pride has been earned. Implicit in my recovery from this characteristic is my acceptance of my humanity. I am human. I am imperfect, and because I am imperfect, I do not have to be a deity, minor or otherwise. That's a relief.

I Am Super Responsible or Super Irresponsible

Here's another one of those twin extreme characteristics. What makes this one particularly dysfunctional is that I'm more likely to be super responsible for the relatively unimportant tasks, like showing up for an appointment on time, and super-irresponsible on the ones that get me into a lot of trouble, like not paying my taxes on time.

Much of my irresponsibility comes as a result of the interplay of some of my other characteristics, like fear of conflict and procrastination. Some of it is just plain bubbleheadedness. I don't stop to think things through, or I will allow myself to be so overstressed that I *cannot* think things through.

One of the neat things about self-help groups is that they teach responsibility at basic levels, like making coffee, or taking up the collection, or just locking up at night. Responsibility is broken down into manageable pieces, and we're not overwhelmed by our tasks. We may not like them, but we do them because we have a commitment to the group, and for the time being the group is more important than our dislike of commitment and responsibility. And then we find that we gain self-esteem by being reliable and responsible. This is new information! Being irresponsible becomes extinguished in favor of being responsible, because the latter feels so much better than the illusion of freedom provided by the former.

Being responsible is living in real time. Being irresponsible is living superficially. Coping with the unpleasant realities of life has its own deliciousness. As our competence in dealing with the slings and arrows of daily life increases, it tastes increasingly good. To be responsible is to cherish independence, and to forgo dependence.

I Am Extremely Loyal Even in the Face of Evidence That the Loyalty Is Undeserved

The only good thing I have to say about this characteristic is that once I figured it out, it was easy to drop.

To put it another way, I was loyal to the wrong people, for the wrong reasons, for much longer than was good for me. I picked the strangest people to be loyal to. Weird, paranoid, psychotic, abusing, seductive, damaging thugs. I identified with perpetrators. I invested everything I had in them: self-esteem, power, love, respect. None of it was ever returned. What's worse, I did it over and over again. My investment would eventually be betrayed. And I would reinvest in the same kind of personality. I picked these people for friends, for mentors, for bosses. I thought one boss had the power to make me or break me. So I gave him that power. When I took my power back, he fired me. Nobody can make me or break me. Only I can do that. So I stopped being an employee, and became my own person. I made my reputation independently of my former boss, and in retrospect, I'm sure that I wouldn't want any reputation that he fostered.

I would give the worst kind of abusive boss 30 days' notice, when I should have given him 30 seconds'.

What became clear was that I was (a) gullible, and (b) a poor judge of character. I was asked what these persons did to deserve my trust, my loyalty or my respect. I had no answer. None of it was earned. Therefore, I owed them nothing. My loyalty only need last as long as the last paycheck. This sounds callous and hard, if not cruel. The alternative is very unpleasant. It's far more important to know when to quit a job, when to get out of a bad marriage, when to retreat from an indefensible position.

Again, this is a control issue. We need to learn how to give up our fear of failure, our need to be liked and our need to hang on forever. Alcoholics Anonymous taught us to respect the paradox that to win we had to surrender. If our lives are ever to become manageable, we must understand that we are powerless over others.

I Look for Immediate as Opposed to Deferred Gratification

Deferred gratification may be the hallmark of middle-class social mobility. I, on the other hand, want what I want when I want it, especially if I have procrastinated too long in doing whatever was necessary to get what I wanted in the first place. Because of this, I have learned not to carry credit cards or too much pocket money.

Sometimes expectations are unreasonable or inappropriate. Authors complain that it took their publisher a year to publish their book, when a two year interval is the industry standard. Customers complain that they didn't get their merchandise overnight, when they live three thousand miles away and only paid for normal shipping. It seems that we expect everybody to drop what they're doing to attend to our needs. Then we get upset when these needs and expectations are not met.

Part of my growing up process has been to understand that others are not there to minister solely to my needs. Everybody else has their own agenda, their own needs and circumstances to consider before my needs will necessarily be met.

To say that patience is a virtue is not good enough. More to the point, why is patience better than getting what I want now? The answer is that life doesn't provide me with what I want on demand. That may seem somewhat unfair. But that's the way it is. I do get what I need, in time's own time. It is better to be patient waiting my turn than to waste my energy throwing a tantrum.

I Lock Myself into a Course of Action without Giving Serious Consideration to Alternate Behaviors or Possible Consequences

Adult children of alcoholics often wonder why they get into trouble with their family, with their peers, and with their employers. If they are recovering in Alcoholics Anonymous or another Twelve Step program, their pain may be particularly acute. After all, they're working their way through the Steps. They have a sponsor and attend meetings on a regular and consistent basis. In short, they're doing all that they're supposed to do. So how come they're being called on the carpet for their behavior?

Nowhere do so many of the characteristics of the adult child come into play than with that exquisite form of manipulation known as the *fait accompli*. The fait accompli, or "thing accomplished" is well established in the COA's repertoire of survival skills. It was created out of necessity, when the young child's every independent action was arbitrarily criticized, negated, and disparaged.

An example: when I was nineteen, I enlisted in the army (my school grades could not compete with my drinking and card playing—the only choice I saw was to leave school, and the army was the only place to go for the untrained and unskilled youth). The army physical, all the testing, and other paperwork was accomplished without the knowledge of my parents or friends. I announced my decision to the family the day before I left for Fort Dix. My friends had perhaps a few days more notice. It was done, engraved in stone. It was useless to try to talk me out of it. Nothing could be changed. No alternatives could be presented or considered. I—and they—were locked into my decision.

My friends and my parents were, appropriately, shocked by my decision. I thought at the time they took it rather well. In retrospect, however, I don't ever remember asking them how they felt about my decision. I didn't want to know.

The adult child thinks—and believes—that if his action is done, the action (and he) will be forever free from criticism. To criticize the adult child's behavior (he believes) is to judge and condemn the person.

Were the adult child to test reality, she would have to deal with the answer(s). She would rather not confront the possibility that she may not do what she wants to do. Much better, she thinks, to guess at reality and to act on her guess than to deal with answers she may not like or to be forced to consider new possibilities or alternate behaviors.

ACOAs often have great difficulty in making decisions. Once having made a decision, however, the ACOA is not inclined to change it, no matter how impulsive or self-defeating the decision may be. The ACOA confuses rigidity with strength and weakness with flexibility. Thus, the ACOA sees rigidity as a virtue rather than a character defect to be submitted to the rigors of the Fourth, Fifth and Tenth Steps.[15]

The combination of virtuous rigidity and fear of confrontation serve to make the ACOA difficult to get along with. Friends and families are outraged by the ACOA's actions, yet don't know how to deal with someone who will not take responsibility for checking out one's actions before they are accomplished. If they do nothing, they have been successfully manipulated and feel cheated and deprived.

Employers and friends would do well not to believe that the fait accompli is, indeed, engraved in stone. Although the ACOA will protest mightily and loudly, with every conviction that he is absolutely and forever right, the fait accompli needs to be undone, and undone at once, preferably by the person who originally executed it. If, as in my case, the action is truly unchangeable, the COA will certainly benefit from knowing how each of his associates feels about the action and the way the decision was arrived at. The ACOA needs to be taught healthy ways of dealing with confrontation; these will not be learned in self-help groups, but in groups facilitated by a well-trained group professional.

Testing reality and accepting the possibility of alternatives is a healthy and intimate way of interacting with life. ACOA's will find that practice of these new skills will help heal the pain that caused the creation of the old survival skills.

This characteristic is symptomatic of Attention Deficit Hyperactivity Disorder (ADHD). Dr. David Comings believes that it is more helpful to see ADHD as a genetic disorder of inhibition that results in inattention, impulsivity, and conduct disorder.[16] Im-

---

15. See appendix 1 for a list of the 12 Steps of Recovery.

16. Comings, David E. *Tourette syndrome and human behavior.* Duarte, CA: Hope Press, 1990.

pulsivity, while a problem, is not a defect of character. When one understands that impulsivity of this type often leads to relapse among alcoholics, one begins to understand the causes of the complexity and intractability of alcoholism, and just how futile it is to blame the alcoholic for relapse. If sober people do not understand alcoholism in all its complex layers, how can we expect the alcoholic to do better?

I Seek Tension and Crisis and Then Complain About the Results

I'm the kind of guy who thrives under crisis. I know just what to do. When my office was torched on Memorial Day morning, I was up and running by five in the evening. I'm always on the edge, keeping the adrenaline flowing. I'm the kind of guy who waits until the last minute to file his income tax, whether or not there's any tax due. Only once did I ever turn in a term paper on time as an undergraduate; I had misinterpreted the due date and sent it in a month too soon. I thought it was due the day I finished it.

It seems that I always needed a crisis or a tension factor to motivate me to do anything important. I now wonder how much of that is due to chronic depression, when every part of me is slowed down. The adrenalin rush was one of my home remedies for depression.

This type of behavior wouldn't be so bad unless it had negative results. Obvious, isn't it? Well, to me it wasn't. I just kept accumulating the consequences, complaining about them, but not taking responsibility for the behavior that started them.

The longer I kept sober, the more I discovered that natural highs were chemically different than adrenaline highs. Adrenaline didn't taste or feel as good, and eventually I sensed that for me it was a bad drug.

I didn't discover stress management until my last year in graduate school. I knew that commuting to New York City for an hour to an hour and a half each way was stressful. I knew that my marriage, my graduate studies and my job were all stressful. What I wanted to do was change them all, believing that if I could get rid of the stressful object, I could get rid of the stress and all its painful consequences. Creating a crisis diverts attention away from me, and on to the crisis itself or on to another person. Unfortunately, none of these coping mechanisms work. Better that they be abandoned in favor of more workable solutions.

I Avoid Conflict or Aggravate It; Rarely Do I Deal With It

Most organisms, from single cell amoebas all the way up to humans, have a fight or flight response to conflict and danger. But it is only humans who have the ability to reason, and to *deal* in different ways with conflict.

For me, any relationship, no mater how benign or innocent, is loaded with potential for conflict. At a friend's house, I would rather read a comic book in isolation than interact with others. I was as much interested in getting even as I was in winning. If there was a way to make an argument go downhill fast, I would find it. When I graduated from college and went into business, I hoped to find a better way to make decisions. I was unsuccessful.

In my family, we solved our relationship problems with violence, both physical and verbal. Whoever got in the last word or whoever achieved the highest decibel count won the argument. Whoever won verbally was at high risk for losing physically. So nobody won, really, and everybody lost. What I lost, more than anything, was a model for resolving conflict in a mature way.

The self-help groups said, "Talk it out." That usually works in a crude, unrefined way. But what I would like to introduce to the self-help community is a wonderful little analysis of healthy ways to confront and to respond to confrontation. Now I for one do not like to be confronted or challenged. I dislike it not just a little, but intensely. It makes me very uncomfortable. I would rather not have to justify whatever it is that I am doing. I do not like being defensive, or being manipulated into a defensive position. Nevertheless, it has become quite apparent over the years that I am not right all the time, and that sometimes my behavior exceeds even being outrageous. Sometimes it's just irritating to others, sometimes it's worse. I have come to understand that it is better to be made aware of inappropriate behavior while it's just irritating, rather than outrageous. So I have a vested interest in being confronted from time to time. It keeps me centered in real time. But how to deal with all those uncomfortable feelings?

Enter Gerard Egan. Egan, in one of my favorite textbooks on interpersonal living,[17] defines confrontation as "anything that invites a person to examine his behavior and its consequences more carefully." That sounds a bit more mature than hitting your opponent over the head with a club. Egan goes on to explain that there are several different kinds of confrontation:

A: INFORMATIONAL CONFRONTATION

This type of confrontation doesn't deal so much with ignorance as it does to invite another to examine new information or misinformation. This book is a good example of informational confrontation. It doesn't tell you that you're stupid. It just invites you to look at new information. You take what you want and leave the rest.

B: EXPERIENTIAL CONFRONTATION

At times, my life experience differs from another person's. I can invite others to look at the differences between my experiences and those of others. If an authority figure, or any other person dismisses your experience as the child of an alcoholic, you may state that your experience was what you lived, that while it may have been unique to you, it nevertheless deserves consideration.

C: STRENGTH CONFRONTATION

This involves telling another person that he or she may have strengths or assets that haven't been considered or used. If one can see personal assets that were previously unrecognized, they may well want to practice or use those assets so much that there is little time or motivation to use behaviors that are less mature or helpful.

D: WEAKNESS CONFRONTATION

Most of us are familiar with pointing out the shortcomings of others. Egan reminds us that this type of confrontation is preferred only by low-level communicators. It really doesn't work that well. Confronter and confrontee are really better off when it is not used.

---

17. Egan, G. (1976). *Interpersonal living.* Belmont, CA: Brooks-Cole.

E. ENCOURAGEMENT TO ACTION

Egan points out that high-level communicators are doers and initiators. You encourage another to act upon their world in some appropriate manner, instead of being passive.

So far, so good. All of these sound so much better than my family's old ways of operating. But my family just never responded well to confrontation. If you got angry at me, I would get angry at you for getting angry at me. This enabled me to avoid the original issue altogether. Egan came up with several healthy ways of confronting, and accepting confrontation.

Egan suggests that confrontation take place tentatively. We avoid absolutes like "always" and "never," and replace them with qualifications that help the other explore the issue more easily. We need to remember that our goal is not to win, to prove a point, or to smash an opponent, but to solve a problem. This is accomplished by not arousing defenses, but through suggestion.

The amount of energy put into a confrontation needs to be proportionate to the strength of a relationship. The more I care about a person, the more effort I will put into a confrontation, and the more care I will take with it. I also need to be able to assess accurately the ability of the person to accept and integrate whatever it is I am saying. If a person is particularly fragile, I need to remind myself that I am not here to break or punish, but to help. This is very important when dealing with children, with clients, and with alcoholics.

My usual ways of responding to confrontation are quite dysfunctional. These are very defensive and unhelpful. They include not thinking about or processing the information that is provided to me, distorting the information received, discrediting the confronter, persuading the confronter to change his or her views, devaluating the importance of the topic in question, rejecting the confrontation, looking for people to support my side, and, most insidious of all, agreeing with the confronter so that he will focus his attention on someone else as soon as possible. This is Egan's list, and I have practiced all of these to perfection.

I have found it very helpful to follow Egan's suggested healthy responses to confrontation. These suggestions help dissipate my fear, maintain my self-esteem and give me a sense of being in control of my situation.

I have a right to understand what a person is saying. Too often, I overreact to a confrontation that is poorly understood. If I do not understand what is going on, or if I am confused, I always have the right to use the resources of others: I may use a group or my support system to help explore the issues. I always have the right to explore the issue I am being confronted with. That does not mean that I have to agree with the confronter. I do have an obligation to myself and to my commitment for growth to explore the issue in all its dimensions. If I determine that the confrontation has merit, either in whole or in part, then my need for moral consistency requires that I change or alter my behavior in some way. I need to understand that it takes time for me to process a confrontation and to work it through. I do not need to jump to another's timetable.

I Fear Rejection and Abandonment: yet I Am Rejecting of Others

As children, many of us were abandoned, if not physically, then symbolically. My father would threaten to leave me with a tribe of Canadian Indians who had, he said, a reputation for abusing and killing their young. Since our family had a long term relationship with the Lake St. Francis Mohawks, and had a young Mohawk woman living with us for a year, my father was credible. I believed him. Much later during my recovery, I realized that this was emotionally abusive behavior, to say nothing of ethnic bias. But I still had no idea how painful this was until I observed another COA jokingly say to his two-year-old son, while taking garbage to the town dump, that he was going to leave him there as well. The child was incapable of seeing this in a funny light, and screamed with terror.

All children have fears of abandonment during the course of their development. It is an age appropriate fear that in healthy families gets worked out as the child grows older. In families affected by alcoholism, however, these fears are never resolved. We continue to act out our abandonment issues by threatening abandonment to those who are close to us.

When I was in my thirties, I discovered backpacking and mountain climbing, practicing both with a passion. Several of my contemporaries had the same interests as I, and I was dying to go with them. My fears of rejection led me to state that I preferred to walk alone. I could not bear the thought of asking to join them and risk rejection. So I guaranteed my rejection in advance by becoming a professional loner. I eventually discovered that I would not be diminished in any way by asking others to join me. Some accepted, some did not. I found that I could cure my rejection complex by doing exactly the opposite of what I was doing before. Instead of rejecting others before they could reject me, I accepted others before they had a chance to accept me. The results were very interesting. Part of my grief work involved dealing with how different my life might have been had I discovered this simple principle early in life, rather than at the threshold of middle age.

I think this may be one reason why we continue to feel different from others. Our tendency to isolate ourselves from other people leaves us spiritually alienated and unconnected. And then we act out our spiritual neediness by doing exactly the opposite of what we need to do to get better.

The eighty/twenty rule of thumb applies here. Eighty percent of the people with whom I become involved like what I do and what I represent. They can usually see beyond my defenses (which are somewhat weaker now) and see the real me.[18] And much to my continuing surprise, I am liked and respected. And then there are the twenty percent who don't like what they see. Personally, I prefer 24-hour standing ovations for whatever I do. But that's probably an unrealistic expectation. Equally inappropriate is being shattered because I am rejected by a minority of my audience. All I need do is remember all that positive feedback I've received over the years, do a quick reality check, and I'm back on course.

Unconditional acceptance is such a wonderfully healing act that I'm surprised nobody gave it a name before Carl Rogers did in the late 1940s. Rogers called it unconditional positive regard. He was soundly criticized for offering it as a therapeutic technique by the psychological establishment at the time. Fifty years later, unconditional positive regard is taught in all the counseling schools.

Unconditional acceptance is a neat way to carry the message of health and recovery to others. By accepting others first, we bring a little healing to other wounded people. These others in turn can

---

18. Hard on the outside, soft on the inside.

take that healing and begin to accept themselves unconditionally. Once that happens, they have something to share. And then the positive, healing cycle continues.

I Fear Failure, but Sabotage My Success

My fear of failure kept me from risking any new venture. What I did not understand was that failure is a gifted and valuable teacher. Let me explain. I failed as a private in the army. I did not become a general (other than a general nuisance), and so paved the way to be successful in other endeavors. Along the way, I have also failed at being a banker, a dishwasher, a lumberjack, a bouncer, a bartender, a truck driver, a librarian, a short-order cook, an administrator, a supervisor. While I may have showed some talent or acquired a little skill in each of these occupations, my failure to rise to the top in any of them inevitably led me to what I am doing now. I have been successful as a clinician and as a bookseller, but I did not discover these occupations early in life. Had I done so, I might have failed at them as well.

So I am grateful for my past failures. They have taught me the benefits of risk. If I risk, I get to discover new talents and exercise old ones in new and creative ways.

But how do I sabotage myself? I am tempted to say, "Let me count the ways," because the number seems so large. But apart from the characteristics listed here, my greatest self-imposed obstacle to success involves projects that are too big, too wide in scope, too involved, too complicated—just too, too much in any dimension.

The cure, it seems, is as simple as "Keep It Simple." For example, I've wanted to write this book for over fifteen years. At one time, I wanted to write the all-time, definitive treatise on children of alcoholics, with exquisite research that would prove all my points and silence all the critics forever. Well, that would have taken me forever, and long before forever came along, I would have lost interest in it. So I took a few ideas that I had, and published them in smaller pieces. These pieces became chapters, and when I had a few chapters assembled in one place, I risked sending them to a publisher. The result is this book, and maybe I have enough written to start another.

I Fear Criticism and Judgment, yet I Criticize and Judge Others

Criticism makes me fall apart. I'm often shattered by it all out of proportion to the actual words used. About the only thing I remember getting praise for as a child was cleaning my plate at the dinner table. This, I am sure, contributed to my eating disorder. But more importantly, I internalized the need for perfection both in self and others. My chronic negativism is a burden both heavy and unnecessary. It disrupts my relationships by making my presence anywhere as attractive and pleasant as a lead brick.

There are some antidotes. The first, which I will go into more depth later in this book, is my use of vitamins. I can deal with criticism much more ably when my nutrition is up. I decompensate easily when my nutritional level is down. I am fragile and easily destroyed by adverse comments about myself or my behavior. When I take my vitamins on a daily basis, I am emotionally stronger and less vulnerable to adverse criticism, whether or not justified.

I need to remind myself that praise brings more behavioral change than blame. If I am as quick to praise as I was to criticize, then my relationships will improve. That takes practice.

I had sometimes seen myself as a rough diamond, but had resisted the cutting and polishing necessary to make an attractive gemstone. One way to acquire a little polish in interpersonal skills is to invite feedback, which is significantly different from criticism. Feedback is commentary about your behavior or work that has been observed by people who are committed to your growth as well as their own. Such persons are usually found in growth or self help groups. Good feedback is delivered in a caring manner. It is brief and specific. It is timely; that is, it concerns current, rather than past behavior. It identifies strengths as well as weaknesses. It is not accompanied by analysis, judgment or theory. The giver, however, may state how your behavior impacts on his or her feelings or behavior. Gerard Egan, in his book *Interpersonal Skills,* offers this example of feedback.

Interpersonally, you are a strong person. By that I mean that you're active. You initiate dialogue with others. You risk yourself by disclosing yourself rather deeply. And yet you don't seem overly anxious when you do any of these things. All of that strikes me as strength. It has two effects on me. It makes me feel good, because you add a dimension of honesty to the group. It also makes me a bit nervous, because you challenge me. What you do invites me to risk myself.[19]

Isn't that exquisite! Isn't that a whole lot better than someone's saying you're a nice person? This kind of feedback feels so good that the person receiving it will bend over backward to practice her newfound strength. And by practicing one's strengths and talents, one finds that character deficits have little choice but to shrink and disappear. That's why, when someone tells me I'm a nice person, I always ask that person to be specific. "Tell me more," I say. "What do you mean by nice?"

Compliments are a gift. I used to not believe them and reject them. It was pointed out to me that I would not do that with any other gift, even if I did not like the color or the size or the manufacturer. I would at least have the good graces to say, "Thank you." So that is what I do when I receive a compliment. The thank you forces me to accept the gift. I do not have to believe it. I can put it up on the shelf and look at it later. But I do accept gifts now, and in the accepting sometimes comes understanding that my gifts and talents do not exist in a vacuum.

Sometimes the feedback I get is so strange or difficult to believe that I have to accept it conditionally. I say, "That's new information to me. I'm finding it a little difficult to understand just right now. I need to process it a little more before I can respond to it. I'll get back to you at our next meeting." Sometimes feedback may be at considerable variance with previous experience, or with concurrent feedback from others. In these cases, my response needs to take these other factors into consideration. It helps to do a little reality checking, and ask others who are close to you to help evaluate the feedback.

I Manage My Time Poorly and Do Not Set My Priorities in a Way That Works Well for Me

I have left this characteristic for the last for a reason. It's the last one I discovered, and the last one being worked on. Time manage-

---

19. Egan, G. (1976). *Interpersonal living*. Belmont, CA: Brooks-Cole.

ment is a source of constant frustration with me. I've considered getting up a petition for another 24-hours in every day, but somehow I can't expect that Creation will be revised just to suit my particular needs.

Part of my problem is that I am a poor judge of time. My memory for time is limited. I can estimate within fifteen minutes how long it will take me to drive 350 miles in any kind of weather because the estimate is based on simple arithmetic. On the other hand, I cannot judge with *any* accuracy how long it will take to perform a task that requires any thought or handling of paper.

I try to sort out my priorities by determining what portion of a task can be accomplished right now. I have learned to delegate, not only downwards, but upwards. When I was a banker, I nearly had a nervous breakdown because I thought that the only way I could delegate was to those employees I supervised. When I discovered that my superiors were paid to handle the problems I couldn't handle, I referred the problems back to them for solution.

Homemakers probably have a better idea of how to manage time than most office managers. While an appliance is performing one task, you do another. The idea is to use another person or machine's energy instead of your own. Back in the sixties, there was a great return-to-the-farm movement, the idea being that one should be self-sufficient in all things. What none of the idealists seemed to realize is that self-sufficiency is inherently inefficient, and is almost always characterized by poverty. There is just so much that one person can do. The same thing, by the way, occurs with emotional self-sufficiency. You can recover on your own and chew up a lifetime and a family or two. Or you can get help and accomplish a lot in a short amount of time. The limits of time and energy determine how much one can accomplish. If one is to have leisure, or to get done all that must be done, one must either learn to use machines wisely or to delegate effectively. Not everything has to be accomplished at once. It is permissible to accomplish our tasks sequentially, one after another. Once the skills needed to perform a new task have been acquired, then one can attempt to do several things at once, often with a fair degree of success.

Time management takes place in real time. That means I have to deal with reality more than I want. I have to spend more time planning, and less time doing. For example, I usually work right up to closing time, and then a bit over. Then I leave, with desk and papers a mess. When I take the time to quit work a half hour early, and clean up my desk, my personal management becomes quite efficient.

3 ...

The Stages of Growth

The first psychology book I ever willingly read was Abraham Maslow's *Toward a Psychology of Being*.[1] Maslow was a good choice. I was early in my recovery as an alcoholic and very impressionable. Maslow provided a philosophy of health that I found far more palatable and helpful for recovery than the sin bias of my youthful education. Maslow was a founder of a school of psychology and a president of the American Psychological Association. Publishing in 1968, he probably knew little of alcoholism and even less of children of alcoholics. Nevertheless, he anticipated the rapid growth of the self-help movement of the eighties when he wrote that "growth is, *in itself*, a rewarding and exciting process." In those persons, he wrote, who are growth-oriented, gratification of the growth instinct results in increased motivation and accelerated pursuit of more growth and self-knowledge.

At about the same time, Elisabeth Kübler-Ross published her developmental model of the stages of death and dying.[2] These are more properly termed stages of growth because they describe how an individual meets and deals with new information and the crisis caused by that information. Dealing with alcoholism, whether it is your own or that of a member of your family is no less a crisis than that of any other life-threatening disorder. It is, then, subject to the

1. Maslow, A.H. (1968). *Toward a psychology of being*. (2nd Ed.). New York: Van Nostrand.

2. Kübler-Ross, E. (1970). *On death and dying*. New York: Macmillan.

same growth dynamics. Perhaps because of the complexities and challenges of alcoholism, confronting and dealing with it presents a remarkable opportunity for growth in the individual.

These stages are developmental in nature. Each stage is better experienced and worked through in sequence before the next is fully integrated. Much growth is lost when one tries to integrate a later stage before addressing the concerns of earlier developmental stages. Thus, the pious Christian may readily forgive his parents for their transgressions, because that is what his church and culture tell him to do. But if he forgives before dealing with his anger, he runs the risk of repressing a catalog of emotions that will inevitably leak out in destructive ways. Conversely, each stage is meant to be worked through so that the next may be addressed. Thus, the person who holds anger precious, feeding and nurturing it obsessively for years, delays if not destroys all opportunities for growth and fulfillment.

This is not to say that there isn't much backing and filling. Like working the Twelve Steps of Recovery, working through each developmental stage comes a little at a time, with a little bit of skipping over here and there as insight and understanding arrive on the heels of hard work.

Getting better is hard work. Hard work, in emotional terms, is doing those things that you don't want to do, even if they're good for you. Hard work is not prayer, incantations, crystals, magic, medications, drugs, or reading a book. Some of these things may be helpful from time to time, but they do not absolve you from the necessity of working hard for your recovery. Hard work is experiencing a feeling to its fullest, trusting that you won't be destroyed by it, trusting that you will come out the other side of the feeling and be OK. Getting better is worked in real time. That's one minute at a time, one day at a time. Fantasy, which preserved our sanity in childhood, now must be put aside as an unhelpful diversion. Hard work is doing what I can do *right now* to get better. Hard work is going to a meeting or to therapy, even though you're depressed, angry, exhausted, tied up with children, or the car won't start. Hard work is attempting the suggestions of your sponsor, your friend or your therapist even though you're sure nothing will work and that their suggestions are just so much silly nonsense. Hard work is letting go when every instinct tells you to hang on for the preservation of your soul. Hard work is sweat and fatigue. Hard work is fear and courage and tears and pain. It's wrestling with one's past and one's present all at the same time, with no indication of what the future will be. Hard work is doing all this and then doing it again. Hard work is doing none of this and then forgiving yourself for not having done it and then doing it anyway. Hard work is a triumph over our defenses, a triumph over our past and a tribute to our present.

Stage 1: Isolation and Denial

Alcoholism is something we don't talk about. We perceive alcoholics as dirty, disgusting, and shameful. We know alcoholism hurts innocent people. It is, in the words of the Veterans Administration and the Supreme Court of the United States, "willful misconduct." We're told that alcoholism is embarrassing, sinful and worthy only of our contempt. As a result, we are subject to the limitations of our own experience and knowledge. We are condemned to rediscover what others have already discovered generations before us. We are condemned to explore again and again the false trails of others and to repeat their errors. We never seem to go on from where others left off.[3]

To make matters worse, when we finally screw up the courage to talk to an alcoholism professional about this loathsome thing, we're told we're in "denial." To be in denial is, once again, to be wrong.

Given the cultural context of alcoholism, I agree with Kübler-Ross, who sees denial as "a healthy way of dealing with the uncomfortable and painful situation which some . . . have [had] to live for a long time." Denial performs a vital function by protecting us from cultural shame. On the other hand, denial interferes with our dealing with the painful and life-threatening realities of alcoholism. If we can rid ourselves of shame, perhaps we will live a little longer and a little better.

There is nothing like confrontation to make us deal with our attitudes, our biases, and our prejudices. My first confrontation with the reality of alcoholism came when my mother, whom I had wished dead, told me she had gone to Alcoholics Anonymous.

I had been living in Westchester, commuting to my job on Wall

---

3. This is contrary to human nature and the nature of language. See Hayakawa, S.I. (1941). *Language in action*. New York: Harcourt, Brace.

Street. My mother had long been divorced from my father and lived in the Hamptons. During the summer of 1971, I spent several weekends with her. She was having difficulties with her job. As a matter of fact, it seemed that every month or so she had a new job. One time I came out, she had her leg in a cast. It was the other driver's fault, she said. Each time I visited her, she asked me to bring a bottle. So I would bring a bottle of good gin—not the rotgut vodka she was drinking—and we would sit on the beach or in her living room swapping stories and gossip. At the beginning of the summer I was bringing the bottle home half full. By the end of summer, the bottle was inevitably empty when it came time for me to leave. It got that way because my mom would disappear into the kitchen every five minutes or so and reappear noticeably drunker. Around Labor Day, I decided that my mother would never get it together, and since I did not want to be responsible for her, it would be better for her to die. And so I resolved not to call her or see her again.

The phone call came a few days before Thanksgiving. It was my mother calling, and I took the call in my bedroom. "I found AA," she said. In the instant of that phone call, I knew what the problem was. All the strange things in my life and the weird behavior of my parents was due to something called alcoholism. Up to this time, I had hardly ever heard of alcoholism, let alone Alcoholics Anonymous. "Thank God," I replied and we made a date to see each other at my grandmother's house for Thanksgiving.

At Thanksgiving, my mother looked real good. She talked good, she smelled good, she dressed good. Mom really had it all together, and I was impressed. She talked a lot about AA and how the "program" changed her life. In fact, all she could talk about was AA, except for the time she suggested I go to Al-Anon, a group set up for the families and friends of alcoholics.

My reply was that she was the one with the alcohol problem and she seemed to have that problem well in hand. So there was no need for me to go to Al-Anon, thank you but no thanks for now. If I ever need it, I'll let you know. I was, however, a bit concerned that my mom, now being converted, would try to convert me too. So I asked if my drinking bothered her. She said no, and I continued pulling on my Molson's and my grandmother continued sipping her whiskey and water and that was the end of that discussion.

A year later, my mother, still sober, informed me that she wanted us to help her celebrate her anniversary in Alcoholics Anonymous. I couldn't help but wonder how one celebrated without drinking and asked her how she proposed to do that. Her answer was to get me to agree to go to her AA meeting and watch her celebrate. I didn't want to go. I didn't like doing things I hadn't done before. I didn't like going where I didn't know anybody. I didn't like meetings. I didn't want to have anything to do with *those people*. I couldn't, however, think of a gracious way out of it. I liked my mother's sobriety, and I was scared to death she would lose it. My wife agreed to accompany me and so I went to my first meeting of Alcoholics Anonymous.

That meeting, like so many others before and since, was held in a church basement. One long table was set up facing several rows of chairs. A coffee pot perked over in the corner with a plate of doughnuts and coffee cake alongside. My mother introduced us to her friends, all of whom seemed to say, "Isn't she terrific!" I mumbled something appropriate, but wondered why my mother's friends didn't know her as well as I did. Although Mom wasn't drinking, she was still a little bit strange and *wonderful* was not a word I would have chosen to describe her.

Soon the meeting began. My mother was up front at that long table, sandwiched by two matrons. The one on the left was younger than the other, about fifty, dressed in white and pearls. I was sure she was filthy rich and I couldn't figure out what she was doing in such a place. The other woman looked as if she'd been run over by a meat truck. She had obviously been through the mill and was probably in the right place.

Clutching my coffee for security, I sat in the back of the room as close to the shadows as I could get. It soon became apparent that I would be spared the ultimate embarrassment of my mother's embarrassing herself in public. The two matrons were going to do all the talking.

And talk they did, for the better part of an hour. First one, then the other. They told their stories, the drinking they did, how they felt about alcohol and how they were recovering. After nearly twenty years, I don't remember a word they said. I do remember coming away from that meeting knowing that I had learned something about alcoholism and people. Whatever attitudes or beliefs I held about alcoholics and alcoholism were challenged, wrenched out of their sockets by the simple testimony of two people who were now what they seemed to be but who were once very, very different. Neither woman had ever been anywhere near skid row. Each had had a significant alcoholic history; one had stopped early and the other late in her drinking career. Neither fit my preconceptions of how alcoholics acted or felt either before or after drinking. They were clearly not temperance advocates. They weren't ashamed of themselves. They weren't preachers or rabble rousers. They didn't care whether I or anybody else drank. They were concerned only about their own recovery from something they believed was a chronic and progressively debilitating disease.

For all that had happened to them, for all that they had done, they seemed to have a peace of mind that I thought belonged only to saints. It would be nice if I could have some of that, I thought.

Elegantly simple, this first AA meeting reframed my previous concepts of alcoholism in less than an hour. Now that is a powerful confrontation!

I have since come to believe that the cure for denial, and indeed, for most of what ails us, is education in the company of others. Part of that education is the reframing of traditional concepts of alcoholism, which I will attempt in a later chapter. Much of denial is pure ignorance. Ignorance is due to lack of education and is neither character defect nor pathology.

Stage 2: Anger

Anger, rage, envy, resentment. All of these belong in Stage 2 territory. This anger is initially different from the old and repressed anger that comes from childhood hurts. It is very much a "now" anger. We begin to understand that alcoholism is the cause of much of our pain. We curse the fates that brought alcoholism to *our* family. We look at other, normal or healthy families, and wonder why we couldn't have been more like them. Everytime we say "Why me?" "Why alcoholism?" we're expressing our anger at the injustices of fate. Anger over the countless hurts inflicted by our parents then bubbles up and spills over. Many observers see ACOAs and ACOA meetings full of hurt and pain and wonder if adult children spend all their time complaining about the past. What observers may not understand is that the expression of pain, hurt, and anger is a developmental process that will run its course.

In addition, the self-help group may not yet have acquired the experience of members who have gone through this stage and who can pass the benefits of their experience on to newer members of the group. The ventilation of feelings provides a catharsis that releases stored energy and allows healing to take place. Much of our anger at this stage is directed toward those persons whom we are only now identifying as perpetrators: persons who have done us harm physically, emotionally, and sexually. It's important for us to understand that each child in the alcoholic family has a life experience that is different from one's siblings. What was an outrage to one child may be perceived differently by another in the same family, or never experienced at all.

Stage 3: Postponement

Postponing the inevitable is a normal, but unrewarding stage. The inevitable dealing with your own alcoholism or that of your family member occurs in real time, not in fantasy or intellectual time. This is the stage where one quibbles about definitions. If Dad is not "really an alcoholic," then I don't have to deal with it or its effect on me. Objections are raised to the "religious" nature of the self-help groups. Intellectualizing the recovery experience is often chosen as a defense, either by engaging in endless debates, or by the purchase and study of books that provide a less confronting way out. For the alcoholic, it may mean one last drink, one last drunk before going to a rehabilitation center or to Alcoholics Anonymous. The adult child will not attempt to go to an ACOA meeting, placing this important work further down on his or her agenda. Nor will the adult child seek professional help to get their alcoholics sober. This stage is full of if-onlies and might-have-beens. The adult child may set greater and more elaborate criteria before taking action. She says, "I will do something about the alcoholism when." This is a little bit like quitting smoking minutes before you're wheeled into the operating theater for a triple bypass.

Stage 4: Depression

Depression in this stage comes from loss rather than genetic or long term depression. Adult children may experience a sense of time lost and wasted, of decades spent in dysfunctional patterns.

Disrupted relationships, the loss of family and the interruption of careers may all be realized. The enormity of alcoholism and its consequences sweep over us. There is some anger here, followed by helplessness. This is a good time to begin teasing apart the downside emotions: loss, grief, sadness, depression.

My passage through this stage was marked by my discovery of child abuse and neglect. I had been facilitating a group of children of alcoholics, who often complained of being abused verbally and physically by their parents, alcoholic and nonalcoholic alike. My attitude was "I survived it, so can you." One evening, the youngest child in our group, a boy of eleven, complained of not being able to talk because his father had hit him in the jaw. After taking the child to the emergency room, I began to query our local social workers as to what constituted child abuse. I did a lot of investigating that summer. I would read a chapter in a book on child abuse, and spend the rest of the evening with tears welled up behind my eyes, but not let loose. (I had not cried since I was a little boy and it would be years before I learned to cry again.) I spent the entire summer reading as much as I could about child abuse, in little digestible pieces, and feeling very sad most of the time. I listened, with a much more sensitive ear, to the children in my charge. My sadness, however, came not from the children I was seeing, but from my own experience as a child. I had never felt sad as a child, only frustrated and angry. My sadness was a new experience, different from depression. It had much to do with the loss of my childhood, my loss of closeness to my parents, and the loss of many should-have-beens.

Much later, I was able to have dinner with my mother and share with her some of those feelings, without needing or expecting an apology or explanation. The sharing was its own resolution. Similarly, I was able to confront my father at a much later date, and tell him that as his child I was entitled to have a relationship with him, and that his drinking so impaired our relationship as to make it an impossible one. This confrontation was for my sake, not his, because it enabled me to move on with my life without guilt.

Stage 5: Acceptance

In the acceptance stage, the adult child is neither depressed nor angry. This is not a happy stage. Losses are mourned. Except for grief, this stage may be almost devoid of feelings. Understanding and acceptance that alcoholism is a disease takes place. Resistance to the idea that alcoholism is the problem disappears. A measure of peace and dignity is achieved. The adult child is no longer ashamed of alcoholism and is able to say *mother* and *alcoholic* in the same sentence without choking on the words. As shame disappears, the adult child is no longer quite so concerned with anonymity and may blurt out that he/she is a member of a self-help group for adult children of alcoholics.

Stage 6: Hope

We never give up hope that our parents will stop drinking and that everything will return to normal. It's something of a shock to find that when they do recover, everything does not get healthy all at once. The rapid recovery we experienced in the first stages of our new development has been replaced by the hard grind of extinguishing the behaviors that do not work for us.

In this stage, we perceive hope of recovery: recovery of feelings, of lost accomplishments, and the acquisition of self esteem. Forgiveness may be seen as a goal on the horizon, but there is recognition that it may be awhile before it is accomplished.

Stage 7: Spirituality

The whole of life is a school for spiritual growth.

—Elisabeth Kübler-Ross

I am untrained and unread in theology and religion. As such, I have no claim to any credential or expertise in this subject whatsoever. Although I am neither atheist nor agnostic, I no longer belong to any organized religion. Nevertheless, some observations may be appropriate.

Spirituality has to do with the soul, the psyche, that spirit or entity by which we recognize the separation of the living from the dead. The soul is an entity different from pure thought and from feelings. From birth the soul requires love and nurturance. Without love and nurturance, the soul dies and becomes separated from the body.

I believe that many, if not most of the persons who comprise the addictions constituency are spiritually alienated. Their souls have been damaged and scarred by addictive disease and its consequences. It doesn't matter whether it was our parents or ourselves who acquired the addiction. The disease has interfered, to a greater or lesser degree, with the ability of the soul to receive the love and nurturance that it requires to live. We have been involuntarily separated from nurturance and love. As a consequence, those of us who are affected by addictive disease are spiritually needy. We are not sick so much as unfulfilled.

One of the reasons I no longer drink alcohol or take other mind-altering drugs is that I believe that the toxicity of alcohol puts an artificial barrier between my soul and my body, and between my *self* and those who would love and nurture that self. I don't swallow lead and mercury for the same reasons.

There are other barriers to spirituality. The holding of past hurts and pains, of anger and hate, of bitterness and recrimination, interfere with the ability of our soul to grow and to receive love and nurturance. The soul must first be filled before it can give. Thus forgiveness, first of self, then of others, is essential to our psychic survival. At some point in our development, and usually it is a later point, we need to let go of these hurts so that we can give to ourselves the nurturance we need.

Some persons have difficulty with the concept of a higher power. I have no problem with higher powers, I deal with them every day. Time is a higher power, and so is a truck coming at me on the wrong side of the road. But the idea of a God is very troublesome. For many of us, the God of our youth was punitive and judgmental. Cross him and you would spend the rest of eternity roasting on a spit. Such an image of a higher power is inconsistent with the values we learn in recovery. We find that our recovery is incompatible with judgmentalism, prejudice, and bigotry, with getting even, with control and with large egos that demand constant feeding. Should we hold our God to a lesser standard than we hold ourselves? I think not.

My own concept of a God has more to do with systems than with theology. Our universe is made up of laws and systems that govern its operation. Little by little, men and women have discovered these laws and systems, and found out how to use the energies in them for their own benefit. My goal is to live in harmony with these laws and systems, wherever I find them. If there is a master plan for our universe, I suspect that it has more to do with a mute creator sitting on the sidelines chuckling to itself whenever we grow a little and do something we couldn't do before. All this in much the same way that a parent encourages a child to walk, since our creator doesn't much care how we learn or who we learn from so long as we learn.

The beauty of this concept is written in AA's Eleventh Step of recovery, where we are to ask only for knowledge of God's will for us and the power to carry that out. That means we don't need to spend our time in hosannas and praises, because God's ego is strong enough not to need them. That means we don't ask for material things, or ask for miracles, or bargain secretly for private agendas. It means that we try to achieve some kind of harmony with the rhythms of the universe. Harmony with the universe cannot be obtained by imposing our will on others, even when we are right. It means we have to let go and wait for the answers to be shown to us. It means we try to have the faith that we will get what we need. It means that we have to trust others to do for themselves.

I'm not so sure that I want to adopt a fatalistic view of my universe. Although I've had my share of gifts and miracles, and I'm grateful for each of them, I believe more in hard work. I do not attribute the good things that have happened to me to magic. I agree with the novelist A. E. Maxwell that the only difference between magic and science is the level of education in the audience. The more I learn, the less likely I am to ascribe a specific happening or sequence of events, good or bad, to outside intervention, divine or otherwise. On the other hand, I've learned not to fight the universe's city hall. From time to time I've been motivated by the pursuit of money, and I've had more than one scheme that was going to put me on Easy Street. At one time I thought my newsletter was going to make me rich. I found that my customers were more interested in the books that I was selling as a sideline in the newsletter than they were in the newsletter. So I de-emphasized the newsletter and my other projects and became a bookseller, much against my will. From time to time, we experience financial crises that threaten our livelihood. Every one of the projects we have started to save our book business has been less than a resounding success. Yet, we're still here. It looks like our primary purpose in life is to share our gifts and talents with the universe by selling books. Is this God's will? I'm not sure. But I sometimes joke out loud that as sure as the Jews are God's chosen people, Perrin & Treggett are God's chosen booksellers.

The development of a healing spirituality is a late-stage development. Because of this, and also because adult children are so gullible, I caution the reader from accepting too quickly any religious conversions, or from placing too much faith in one guru or another.

Here are my criteria for determining whether or not a particular movement or therapist may be good or bad for my growth and development. When I talk about "my program of recovery," I refer to those choices I have made or behaviors I have adopted in order to regulate the conduct of my life.[4]

1. Can I understand what they are talking about? If their literature is full of made up words I can't find in the simplest of dictionaries, this is a group I don't need. Take any paragraph in their literature at random. Does it make sense to me? Is it babble or understandable? If it can't be understood by someone with an eighth grade education, then the chances are they don't understand what they're talking about either. Robert Jay Lifton calls this "loading the language."[5]

2. Do they attempt to deprive me of any bodily function? I won't even get into an argument if I'm hungry, sleepy, or have to go to the bathroom. If somebody needs to deprive me of my body functions in order to make a spiritual point, then I look elsewhere for enlightenment.

3. Does the group do *anything* to damage my self-esteem, or to set me apart from the rest of my universe? Does it make me look funny,

---

4. Many of these criteria are adapted from Welwood, J. (1987). On spiritual authority: genuine and counterfeit. In Anthony, D., Ecker, B., & Wilberg, K. (Eds.). *Spiritual choices.* (pp 283–304) New York: Paragon House.

5. Quoted in Hassam, S. (1988). *Combatting cult mind control.* Rochester, VT: Park Street Press.

ridicule me, humiliate me, shave my head, expose my life or health to danger, or dress me in strange clothes? None of these things are in my best interests and I need not tolerate them at all. Does the group or its leaders perform, encourage, or tolerate physical, emotional, verbal, or sexual acts of violence or aggression against any person? These actions are precisely what I am trying to recover from. I do not need to repeat the patterns of my dysfunctional history.

4. Do they claim to hear the voice of God, or to speak for Him (Her, It)? Most of us talk to God, but it is mostly schizophrenics who claim to hear God talk to them. Insight can be claimed to be the will of God only at great risk of grievous error.[6] I suspect that those who are not psychotic and who claim to speak for God are trying to manipulate and control me. Part of my recovery is that I no longer allow anyone to control or manipulate me as a matter of principle. By the same token, I try to extinguish my own manipulative and controlling behaviors whenever I recognize them.

5. Does the group allow or encourage its leader or members to gratify their sexual or power needs/desires with other group members? My recovery program states that I will not allow myself to be used or abused by any person.

6. Does the group discourage free inquiry into its methods, ceremonies, teachings, and beliefs? Keeping secrets is part of my dysfunctional history, and I cannot allow myself to perpetrate or perpetuate that dysfunction elsewhere.

7. Is the group open to reason and argument? If not, I will never have a voice in its operation, nor will I be able to compare it with other groups.

8. Does the group have a permanent authority figure? History shows us that benign governments guarantee the regular rotation

---

6. Not every inner voice or insight is of divine guidance. See, for example, the experience of Bill W. (pp 100–101) in [Wilson, W.G.]. (1957). *AA comes of age.* New York: Alcoholics Anonymous World Services, Inc.

of leadership, and that destructive governments invest their authority in a permanent master figure whose only purpose is to dominate members of the group.

9. Does the group offer to integrate me into the rest of society, or does it isolate me from it? Isolation is an integral part of my disease. If I am to recover from it, I need to have access to continuing contact with members of my universe.

10. Does the group or its leaders violate its own teachings? My program of recovery prefers moral consistency over hypocrisy.

11. Does the group use or advocate the use of mind or mood-altering substances to achieve its spiritual goals? This is different from permitting or having no opinion on social drinking of beverage alcohol. While the use of peyote might be appropriate in the Native American Church, and wine in Christian and Jewish ritual, I have chosen to avoid these substances because I have demonstrated repeatedly that they do not work for me, and are, in fact, toxic for both my mind and body.

12. Are the group's leaders teachers or preachers? Teachers share their experience and learning and hope that I will benefit sufficiently from their presence to surpass them. Preachers pump me up and manipulate my emotions. Teachers let me go. Preachers try to hold on to me.

13. Does the group require or pressure me to give all or a portion of my material possessions to the group? It is one thing to advocate nonmaterialistic values and poverty as a precursor or condition of enlightenment or salvation. It is quite another to be manipulated into enriching a power structure that preaches poverty for all but its own leaders. I choose to give my time and money first to my family, and only when their needs are satisfied do I choose to donate to others whose needs may be greater than my own.

14. Lastly, I am concerned about arrogance and rigidity, two characteristics I have been trying to eliminate from my own daily life. It is arrogant and rigid to require members of a group to

profess every tenet of a particular faith. I prefer to take what I want and to leave the rest for others.

Stage 8: Resolution

Resolution occurs when the perpetrators in your life have been successfully confronted and your power has been returned to you. Once resolution has been accomplished, you will be immunized for life against the feelings of powerlessness and helplessness you once had.[7] As Beverly Engel has pointed out, "You will need to find your own way of confronting your perpetrator and anyone else who abused you, betrayed you, or set you up. . . . The method of confrontation is not nearly so important as is your finding a way to do it."[8] I have acted as a surrogate perpetrator in half a dozen role-plays and psychodramas, as well as facilitating confrontations between survivors and parents. No matter what role I take, it is always an emotionally exhausting experience for both myself and the other players. The intensity of the experience is as awesome as the restoration it engenders. Because resolution is such an important stage of growth, I strongly suggest that confrontation of perpetrators not be undertaken unless one is aware of the guidelines put forth in Beverley Engel's *Right To Innocence,* or unless one has the assistance of a helping professional experienced in such matters.

Stage 9: Getting on with It

I think it was Father Joseph Martin who first said it's not what you say at meetings that determines the quality of your recovery, but what you do between them. Likewise, there comes a time in your life when there are more important things than self-help meetings, thereapy, and recovery books. Now all good recovering alcoholics know that only people who go to meetings know what happens to people who don't go to meetings.[9] In the early stages of recovery, attendance at as many self-help meetings as you can

7. Seligman, M.E.P. (1974). *Helplessness on depression, development and death.* New York: WH Freeman.

8. Engel, B. (1990). *The right to innocence.* New York: Ballantine.

9. They relapse.

manage accelerates and affirms recovery. But as recovery progresses, time spent at your regular meetings and in other forms of therapy inevitably diminishes.

If, for example, you have heard everything there is to hear in your AA group, you may want to try ACOA. If ACOA is boring you as a result of too much repetition, you may want to experiment with a Co-Dependents Anonymous or other self-help group for which you may qualify.

The same thing with self-help books. You can read just so many instruction manuals on swimming before you understand that you can't learn to swim from a book. You have to get into the water and start thrashing about.

In the last five years of my recovery, my tastes and interests have changed. Much to my surprise, I have become a family man instead of running away from my relatives. My reading has changed from books on family therapy to those on Native American and political history. Where I used to allow myself one novel between Christmas and New Year's, I now read mysteries by the dozen.

A long time ago, I decided that I would settle for nothing less than full membership in the human race. I was determined that I would submit neither to discrimination nor to disease. The whole of life is my birthright, and I claim it.

The really neat thing about my recovery has been the discovering of talents and qualities that had lain dormant for decades. To my very great surprise, I found that many of these gifts came from my parents, who had demonstrated and modeled them to me as a child.

For over a decade now, getting up and going to work in the morning has been a pleasure rather than a dreaded curse. I am doing what I want to do, and can't imagine myself doing anything else. That's not to say that I don't have my share of dreams and fantasies, but they're all logical extensions of what I am already doing. My wife is first my friend and then my business partner. The older I get, the less I care about money and material possessions, and the more I care about family and the quality of our lives. True wealth can be measured only in those terms, and in those terms I am rich beyond my wildest dreams.

4

The Big Bad Wolf Defined

It's hardly fair to write about children of alcoholics, either adults or kids, until you and I come to some understanding of what I believe alcoholism to be. I apologize for embarking on such a lengthy side trip, but there has been so much drivel published on the subject that it has interfered with a lot of recoveries, both of alcoholics and their children.

Belief is the key word here. Alcoholism, like any other social problem, doesn't exist in real time until and unless you believe it exists. Of course, it can kill you anyway, whether or not you believe it exists. How's that for paradox?

My beliefs about alcoholism are based on my personal experience with alcoholism. By my own definitions, I have alcoholism.

Knowing I have written that I am an alcoholic, you may believe several things about me. Your beliefs about alcoholism may define how you will deal with me even before you have met me and formed an opinion based on personal knowledge of my character. In terms of my relationship with you, that may turn out to be a problem. Even more problematical is how your beliefs about alcoholism influence your reaction to your own alcoholism or your reaction to the alcoholism of those close to you.

I *believe* that the condition I call alcoholism is a disease of genetic origin. That means that I believe I inherited a set of genes from one or both parents that defined how I would respond to beverage alcohol. To say that a disease is genetic does not mean that everybody in the family will get it. Genetics just doesn't work that way.[1] My belief is based on my examination of how beverage alcohol acts in *my* body and influences *my* mind when I drink. My belief is supported by the comparison of my alcohol experiences with the alcohol experiences of others. My belief is further supported, in part, by medical and historical literature that I have carefully selected—none of which *proves* anything. I'm still talking about *beliefs*.

Let's look at the foundations upon which my beliefs about alcohol rest.

When we talk about disease, we are talking about a belief system. A disease is not a disease unless people think it is. For example, the Mano tribe of Liberia does not believe that malaria is a disease because most people have it.[2] Disease, by definition, is an *abnormality*. Malaria in Liberia is too common, too *normal*, to be considered a disease. It's possible that alcoholism has previously had difficulty being recognized as a disease in America precisely because it is so widespread. However, most people in America now seem to believe that alcoholism is a disease. By 1987, 87 percent of Americans polled by the Gallup Organization believed that alcoholism is a disease, up from 79 percent in 1982.[3] In spite of their believing that alcoholism is a disease, Americans indicated that "the exact meaning of 'disease' remains unclear in the public mind," according to a Gallup survey taken in 1988. Although those polled confirmed that they agreed alcoholism was a disease, 31 percent felt that alcoholism was a mental problem, 23 percent felt that it was due to lack

---

1. For a general discussion of the genetics of disease, see Gormley, M.V. (1989). *Family diseases are you at risk?* Baltimore: Genealogical Publishing Company.

2. Alland, A., Jr. (1970). *Adaptation in cultural evolution: an approach to medical anthropology.* New York: Columbia University Press,

3. Gallup, G., Jr. (1987). *Alcohol Use and Abuse in America* (Gallup Report No. 265). Princeton, NJ: The Gallup Organization. Most statistics on alcoholism tend to be based on methodology that is either naive or corrupt. For this reason, the only statistics in this book, other than the number 1, upon which the reader may rely with any degree of certainty, are those published by the Gallup Organization. All others are seat-of-the-pants guesstimates or otherwise suspect.

of willpower, and 16 percent thought that it was a moral weakness.[4]

Taber's Cyclopedic Medical Dictionary begins by stating that a disease is

> Literally the lack of ease; a pathological condition of the body that presents a group of clinical signs and symptoms and laboratory findings peculiar to it and which sets the condition apart as an abnormal entity different from other normal or pathological body states.[5]

The problem is that most people *think* of disease as something communicable, either by virus or by germ. The fact is that there are many kinds of diseases you will recognize that do not fall into the germ/virus kind of disease. For example, all genetic diseases and most metabolic diseases have nothing to do with germs or viruses. They have to do, instead, with an inability to manufacture or process the body chemicals necessary to live efficiently.

Again, Taber's *Dictionary* helps to clarify exactly how a disease differs from other disorders:

> The concept of disease may include the condition of illness or suffering not necessarily arising from pathological changes in the body. There is a major distinction between disease and illness in that the former is usually tangible and may even be measured, whereas illness is highly individual and personal, as with pain, suffering, and distress. A person may have a serious disease such as hypertension but no feeling of pain or suffering, and thus no illness. Conversely, a person may be extremely ill, as with hysteria or mental illness, but have no evidence of disease as measured by pathological changes in the body.[6]

This concept is important because of its application to alcoholism. An alcoholic at the earliest stage of his or her disease has no

---

4. Gallup, G., Jr. and Gallup, A. *Alcoholism Widely Viewed as a Disease But Opinion Diverges on Root Causes.* The Gallup Poll, April 24, 1988.

5. Thomas, C.L. (Ed). (1989). *Taber's cyclopedic medical dictionary.* (16th Ed.). Philadelphia: F.A. Davis Company.

6. Ibid.

pain or suffering, and thus no illness. The disease is thus *invisible*. Implicit in this concept is the idea that one can be alcoholic without being physically or psychologically dependent upon alcohol. I will come back to these ideas in the next chapter, where I will try to make the disease in its earliest stages visible to all.

In the meantime, definitions of alcoholism keep changing. In 1976 this definition was published in the *Annals of Internal Medicine*, and has been widely used ever since.

> Alcoholism is a chronic, progressive, and potentially fatal disease. It is characterized by tolerance and physical dependency or pathologic organ changes, or both-all the direct or indirect consequences of the alcohol ingested.[7]

The World Health Organization (WHO) wants to replace the word alcoholism with the phrase *alcohol drug dependence*, and define that as follows:

> Drug dependence of the alcohol type may be said to exist when the consumption of alcohol by an individual exceeds the limits that are accepted by his culture, if he consumes alcohol at times that are deemed inappropriate within that culture, or his intake of alcohol becomes so great as to injure his health or impair his social relationships.[8]

More recently, a committee of the American Society of Addiction Medicine suggested the following definition:

> Alcoholism is a disease characterized by continuous or periodic: impaired control over drinking, preoccupation with the drug alcohol, use of alcohol despite adverse consequences, and distortions in thinking, most notably denial.[9]

This last definition is the best of a bad lot, but, in my opinion, remains incomplete. The problem is that most definitions tend to

---

7. Staff. (1990, March-April). *ASAM News*. pp. 1, 9.

8. Mendelson, J.H. and Mello, N.K. (1985). *The diagnosis and treatment of alcoholism*. (2nd ed.). New York: McGraw Hill.

9. Staff. (1990, March-April). *ASAM News*. pp. 1, 9.

confuse what happens long *after* the disease is well established rather than what happens *before*.

Let's look at some of the characteristics of alcoholism that fall into other known disease categories, and that describe what happens before the disease has run its course.

Alcoholism is a *familial* disease. It has been observed over more than 20 centuries that alcoholism runs in families. Over the last few decades, we have come to recognize that most alcoholics have at least one family member who is also alcoholic. Half of all alcoholics are children of alcoholic parents. Most of the other half have a grandparent or other relative who is alcoholic. The rare exceptions are either adopted or, if you agree with my beliefs, genetic mutations. But running in families doesn't mean that something is genetic. As Donald Goodwin has pointed out many times, speaking French runs in families, but it doesn't mean that speaking French is of genetic origin.[10]

Nevertheless, any definition of alcoholism must account for the familial nature of alcoholism. It's interesting to note that when family histories[11] are taken over several generations, and the facts of alcoholism are known in each generation, that alcoholism has a tendency to run along gender lines. Thus, the son whose father and paternal grandfather are alcoholic is most likely to be alcoholic. The daughter whose mother and maternal grandmother are alcoholic is most likely to be alcoholic. Just to confuse matters further, families may have gender limited alcoholism in both sexes in the same family. In my family, for example, there are more alcoholics than nonalcoholics of either gender.

Alcoholism is often described as *chronic* disease, meaning that its visible onset is slow and that it lasts for a long period of time. I believe that the earliest, initial symptoms of alcoholism are generally unrecognized except in retrospect. I also believe that there is no invisible line to be crossed. Alcoholism's progressively worse nature is probably a factor of the effects of aging combined with the

10. Goodwin, D.W. (1988). *Is alcoholism hereditary?* New York: Ballantine.

11. The single best mechanism for taking a psychological, medical and emotional history of a family is the genogram. See Marlin, E. (1989). *Genograms*. Chicago: Contemporary. Doing a genogram of your family is an important recovery task for all adult children. Also useful is McGoldrick, M. & Gerson, R. (1985). *Genograms in family assessment*. New York: W.W. Norton.

increasing toxicity of alcohol and its by-products over time. It's chronicity is due to the fact that no genetic disease gets better or disappears. Genetic diseases are always there because the disease is as much a part of our genetic makeup as is the color of our eyes. As such, it is also as much a part of our identity as any other feature that is genetically controlled.

If alcoholism is a genetic disease, it is probably a *metabolic* disease and also probably a *vitamin deficiency* disease. This means that alcoholism involves to some degree the inadequate intake or absorption of factors such as vitamins, minerals or amino acids. Roger J. Williams, the discoverer of vitamin B6, suggested thirty years ago that alcoholism was a vitamin and amino acid deficiency disease.[12] Although nutritional deficiencies are also part of the aftereffects of the disease, as in peripheral neuropathy and Korsakoff's syndrome, it's important to note that I will be suggesting that nutritional deficiency is *one* of the *causes* of alcoholism, rather than a consequence of it.

I will begin with the working hypothesis that *alcoholism is a familial disease, marked by chronicity, and probably caused by metabolic dysfunction or nutritional insufficiencies.* This is by no means a perfect definition, but it is a definition that describes the earlier stages of alcoholism, rather than its later, or terminal stages.

---

12. Williams, R. J. (1981). *The prevention of alcoholism through nutrition.* New York: Bantam; Williams, R J. (1959). *Alcoholism the nutritional approach.* Austin: University of Texas Press.

5 ...

The Big Bad Wolf Redefined

Quite frankly, I'm unhappy about any of these definitions, including my own working definition. They are singularly unhelpful. None help explain to me my physical reactions to beverage alcohol. They don't explain *why* I became alcoholic. They don't tell me *when* I became alcoholic. They don't tell me how my consumption or behavior differs from those persons who are demonstrably not alcoholic. They don't tell me what has to change in order for my alcoholism to cease being a problem. They don't tell me how I could have prevented my alcoholism, and they don't provide clues as to how I might prevent alcoholism in my offspring.

If one listens to many hundreds of life histories of alcoholic drinking, several themes or patterns tend to emerge. My own history follows some of these patterns rather closely.

Let's proceed logically, and see what happens. Genetics always precedes learning. Physiology must be explained before it can be dismissed in favor of learned behavior, wilful misconduct or sin.

With this in mind, my own story has some relevance. At some point in the four-year period before I stopped drinking, I became quite convinced that both of my parents and my mother's mother were alcoholic. I inferred from this observation that, with three close relatives being alcoholic and if alcoholism were hereditary, I was next in line. (I knew I wasn't adopted.) Therefore, I reasoned further, I could prevent getting alcoholism if I controlled my drinking. And that's exactly what I did for several years, with great success. I did most of the things that behavioral scientists recom-

72

mended, although I thought them up myself.[1] The results were that I drank less, I got drunk less, and the periods between my intoxications were greater in length. I no longer drove my car while drunk. There were, however, a few minor problems with my control. The control process required tremendous amounts of energy. The more successful my attempts at control, the more irritable and unhappy I became. When I did drink, I could not predict whether or not I would get drunk, and in fact, I often got drunk against my will. It occurred to me that this was a phenomenon that warranted further investigation. It appeared that, in the words of the First Step of Alcoholics Anonymous, I was powerless over alcohol.

It was suggested to me that if I could drink two drinks every night, no more and no less, then I was not an alcoholic.[2] I rejected this suggestion out of hand. I knew that for me such a limit was impossible. I knew that once I started, most often I did not stop. I was never a social drinker. I was almost always a social drunk. And so I continued my investigations.

One of the first things that I discovered was that historically, whenever I controlled the amount of alcohol consumed, I did not stop. When my father offered me sips of his beer when I was a little boy, he controlled the quantity to be consumed. When I bought the beer, I got drunk. Any attempts to teach me how to drink were doomed to failure.

The next thing that I found in my research of my life history was that I had an enormous capacity for beverage alcohol. I could drink awesome quantities of alcohol without appearing intoxicated. I was the guy who drove the rest of the drunks home from a party. I was the one who had a "hollow leg." I could hold my liquor better than anyone I knew, and I practiced that a lot.

The third item encountered in my history was my record of

---

1. One behavioral scientist once suggested that alcoholics zap themselves in the heinie with a cattle prod every time they thought of drinking. The book *Living sober*, published by Alcoholics Anonymous, offers many suggestions on how to avoid drinking that are significantly more workable and healthy.

2. This is known to medicine as Anstie's limit of not more than 1.5oz of absolute alcohol consumed per day with meals, being the amount calculated in 1874 by Francis Anstie that an adult male could consume without adverse effect to his health. Keller, M., McCormick, M. & Efron, V. (1982) *A dictionary of words about alcohol*. (2nd Ed). New Brunswick, NJ: Rutgers Center of Alcohol Studies.

relapse. That is, I would discover a benefit from not drinking, remark on the benefit, and decide not to drink. Then I would drink anyway. Despite my previously successful termination of nicotine addiction, I never made the connection between successful non-drinking and total abstinence.

All of this was sufficient to convince me that I had a problem with alcohol, and not wanting to repeat my family's history, I sought treatment for alcoholism. I've been sober ever since the tender age of thirty-two.

As part of my treatment, I found myself in a group of teenage alcoholics.[3] I thought to myself that if I was an alcoholic at the age of thirty-two, and my young friends were alcoholic at the age of thirteen and fourteen, then the answers to the causes of alcoholism were not to be found through the examination of aged and cirrhotic derelicts,[4] but in the life histories of young alcoholics. Unfortunately, most of the young alcoholics I knew were also users and abusers of drugs other than alcohol. This would have confounded any research study. I therefore decided to concentrate my research on the one person to whom I had unlimited access—myself.[5]

I spent the better part of two years of lunch hours going through the book and journal stacks at the Mid-Manhattan Branch of the New York Public Library. At the time, most research on alcoholism and on children of alcoholics was not indexed properly. One way to find gems of research was to take each volume of a journal and examine each article for relevant material. In this way, I accumulated a significant body of research, and a solid respect for several scientists, among them Donald Goodwin.

I had read with great interest Goodwin's book, *Is Alcoholism Hereditary?*,[6] first published in 1976, shortly after I got sober and

---

3. Emotionally, we were the same age.

4. Much of the published research on alcoholism at this time used active, skid row alcoholics as research subjects. This type of research is now considered ethically offensive because such alcoholics are incapable of informed consent.

5. I may be the last pot virgin in America. My personal use of mood-altering drugs has been limited to alcohol, nicotine, caffeine and sugar. I attribute this to blind luck rather than to any moral virtue.

6. Goodwin, D. W. (1976). *Is alcoholism hereditary?* New York: Oxford. A revised, second edition was published by Ballantine in 1988.

was familiar with his very original research about adopted-out sons and daughters of alcoholics.

Briefly, Goodwin and his associates discovered that children who were adopted away from their alcoholic parents into nonalcoholic homes immediately after birth were much more likely to become alcoholic than people in the general population. These findings, and the studies that followed, suggested that the influence of heredity was dominant over the influence of environment in alcoholism. Perhaps because the research design was so original, the findings have stood up over the better part of a decade and a half of rigorous examination.[7]

It was with much excitement that I stumbled across Goodwin's review of the literature on heredity published in 1979.[8] What made this literature review stand out from a host of other reviews was Goodwin's hypothesis on familial alcoholism. Goodwin posed the novel question that *if alcoholism was hereditary, what is inherited?* What was even more relevant to me was Goodwin's discussion of the core features of alcoholism. These were (1) loss of control, (2) tolerance, and (3) tendency to relapse. Goodwin did not explicitly state that these three factors were passed from one generation to another. Rather, he theorized that these were environmental and genetic factors which influenced one another.

Because they fit so well into my own experience, both personal and clinical, I've modified Goodwin's hypothesis somewhat, based again on my own perceptions of Goodwin's core features.

One of my first new awarenesses in sobriety was that my wife of ten years had never been drunk. In spite of having accompanied me in numerous intoxications, she herself had never become intoxicated. She was always a cheap date, and I invariably finished her

---

7. Goodwin, D. W., Schulsinger, F., Hermansen, L., Guze, S. B., and Winokur, G. (1973). Alcohol problems in adoptees raised apart from alcoholic biological parents. *Archives in General Psychiatry*. 28, 238–243. For a critique, see Collins, R. L., Leonard, K. E., and Searles, J. S. (1990). *Alcohol and the family: research and clinical perspectives*. New York: Guilford Press, as well as Windle, M. and Searles, J. S. (1990). *Children of alcoholics, critical perspectives*. New York: Guilford Press.

8. Goodwin, D. W. (1979). Alcoholism and heredity. *Archives in General Psychiatry*. 36, 57–61. More readily accessible is his summary of the same concepts in Goodwin, D. W., (1990) Genetic determinants of reinforcement from alcohol. In Cox, W. M. (Ed.) *Why people drink, parameters of alcohol as a reinforcer*. New York: Gardner Press 37–50.

drinks myself. At some point in my nondrinking career, I read a suggestion that alcohol researchers were wasting their time asking why alcoholics drank. It would be far more fruitful to ask them why they did not.[9] When I asked that question of my clients, I received some very illuminating answers.

When nonalcoholics are asked why, in any given drinking episode, they stop drinking, their answers fall into several broad categories: Fear and dislike of alcohol, fear and dislike of intoxication, fear and dislike of future consequences, fear of intellectual or physical impairment, fear or dislike of losing control, fear or dislike of physical reaction to alcohol, intellectual reasons, psychological toxicity or reaction formation, and satiation. Many of these responses, we now know, are due to the phenomenon we call oriental flush syndrome. According to Cohen, "the flush may vary from a mild reddening of the skin around the mouth to severe flushing over the upper third of the body. Symptoms like dizziness, sleepiness, pounding in the head, and nausea are apt to accompany the cutaneous manifestations."[10]

Most nonalcoholic responses came as a surprise to me, a longtime devotee of hard drinking. Most were substantially different from my own responses. In this I was not alone. Alcoholics have been saying for over a century that their drinking was different from nonalcoholics. John B. Gough, an alcoholic writing in 1869, deplored the unjust judgment of those who did not understand that alcoholics were constituted differently than others.[11]

Nonalcoholics simply do not want to lose control of mind or body or feel out of control in any way due to their consumption of alcohol. They fear loss of control, and fear it intensely. They are afraid they won't be able to stop drinking, and monitor their consumption very carefully. They do not want to become too high, and if they become so, they quit drinking immediately.

I suspect that most (nonalcoholic) researchers assume that alcoholics had, at one time, this kind of control over their drinking, and

---

9. I regret that I did not retain the source of this concept.

10. Cohen, S. (1985). *The substance abuse problems.* (Vol 2.) *New issues for the 1980s.* New York: Haworth Press.

11. Gough, J. B. (1869). *Autobiography and personal recollections of John B. Gough.* Springfield, MA: Bill, Nichols & Co.

that as a result of crossing over some imaginary and invisible line, had lost control.[12] E. M. Jellinek stated this explicitly: "Loss of control does not emerge suddenly but rather progressively. . . It becomes fully established several years after the first intoxication."[13] It followed that if one could determine that line, one could re-learn control, and drink again without losing control.

I suggest that alcoholics never have this kind of control in the first place.[14] In fact, alcoholics *like* rather than dislike being out of control. Being out of control, that is, intoxicated, holds no fear for the alcoholic. Being out of control is, instead, a source of pleasure, something to be sought rather than avoided. From time to time, being out of control may be a source of annoyance or inconvenience for the alcoholic. At such times, the alcoholic may tend to mediate or moderate his or her drinking. The alcoholic, following the first intoxications, tries to *learn* how to control his or her drinking. Some alcoholics spend a lifetime trying to learn how to drink. At some later time, in the presence of physical or psychological addiction, the alcoholic discovers that inconvenience disappears as a barrier to lack of control. What was once able to be controlled at will, through learning, is now no longer able to be controlled. Hence, loss of control. The nonalcoholic isn't required by his or her genetic makeup to resort to such extraordinary measures.

Semantic differences in language become very important here. I am suggesting that alcoholics drink differently from non-alcoholics from the very beginning of their drinking careers. They do not develop loss of control. They never had it to begin with. They *lack* rather than *lose* control. To put it another way, alcoholics lack an off switch for their drinking.

Look at another set of responses from nonalcoholics. Non-alcoholics are easily satiated when they drink alcohol. Their satia-

---

12. It is unrealistic to expect members of the one group to comprehend the drinking behavior of the other group—and therein, I believe, lies the cause of the many misconceptions, myths and blind alleys that nonalcoholics have about alcoholic drinking.

13. Jellinek, E.M. (1960). *The disease concept of alcoholism*. New Haven: Hillhouse Press.

14. Some support for this notion will be found in Brown, S. (1985). *Treating the alcoholic; a developmental model of recovery*. New York: John Wiley.

tion response to beverage alcohol is exactly the same as it is to any other beverage. They stop drinking alcohol because they want to, because they don't want any more, because they know when enough is enough, when they no longer enjoy it, when they are satisfied with the amount they've had. All their controls are internal. They have an internal off switch that controls their consumption of alcohol, and this off switch is a biological, rather than a cognitive or thinking, response. If it is a biological switch, it cannot be learned or unlearned.

Alcoholics, on the other hand, stop drinking for reasons that are monotonously external. Listen to these responses: "I don't, I never stopped, I pass out, I ran out, I was thrown out, because the bars close, I stop when exhausted, when I got too drunk, because I didn't have any more money, the party ended, I couldn't see straight, throw up, smoke pot, get too sleepy, arrested, incarceration, jails, funny farms, no money, no friends, when I can no longer function at all." There is never a hint of control, of biological satiation. Control never existed. It wasn't there to lose. Had they drunk orange juice in the same manner as they drank alcohol, we would have thought them very strange indeed.[15]

This has nothing to do with craving, another misconception. Craving has everything to do with physical or psychological addiction.[16] Beginning alcoholics do not crave alcohol.[17] Alcoholics

---

15. It's only fair to note that I have exactly the same reaction to chocolate chip cookies as I do to alcohol. Once I start, I do not stop until I have consumed all that are available, despite intense feelings of guilt and remorse. It is possible, and I make the suggestion, that alcohol specific satiation has much to do with the metabolism of sugar.

16. Psychological addiction can last a lifetime, whereas physical addiction may end with the detoxification period. For example, I am psychologically addicted to wearing clothes in public. Although in extreme circumstances I might be persuaded to do without clothes in public, I would be extremely uncomfortable. At the very first opportunity, I would put my clothes back on. My experience with nicotine addiction, which was a heavier physical addiction than my alcohol addiction, indicates that there is memory for the benefits of smoking even after decades of total abstinence. But such cravings, if they can be called that, last only for extremely small fractions of a second. During the detoxification period, such cravings were intense and seemed to be endless. They were, however, progressively limited in duration as the time between the present and the last fix increased.

17. Beginning alcoholics, as I suggest elsewhere, may be expressing an unconscious desire to feel normal, integrated, together. etc.

demonstrate unsatiated responses to beverage alcohol often from their very first drink, unlike nonalcoholics. Rather than craving a drink, they simply don't stop drinking unless some outside factor intervenes.

Listen to Jack London's description (first published in 1913) of his first drink of beverage alcohol, which was also the occasion of his first drunk:

> I was five years old the first time I got drunk. It was on a hot day, and my father was plowing in the field. I was sent from the house, half a mile away, to carry to him a pail of beer. 'And be sure you don't spill it,' was the parting injunction.
>
> It was, as I remember it, a lard pail, very wide across the top, and without a cover. As I toddled along, the beer slopped over the rim upon my legs. And as I toddled, I pondered. Beer was a very precious thing. Come to think of it, it must be wonderfully good. Else why was I never permitted to drink of it in the house? Other things kept from me by the grown-ups I had found good. Then this, too, was good. Trust the grown-ups. They knew. And anyway, the pail was too full. I was slopping it against my legs and spilling it on the ground. Why waste it? And no one would know whether I had drunk or spilled it.
>
> I was so small that in order to negotiate the pail, I sat down and gathered it into my lap. First I sipped the foam. I was disappointed. The preciousness evaded me. Evidently it did not reside in the foam. Besides, the taste was not good. Then I remembered seeing the grown-ups blow the foam away before they drank. I buried my face in the foam and lapped the solid liquid beneath. It wasn't good at all. But still I drank. The grown-ups knew what they were about. Considering my diminutiveness, the size of the pail in my lap, and my drinking out of it with my breath held and my face buried to the ears in foam, it was rather difficult to estimate how much I drank. Also, I was gulping it down like medicine, in nauseous haste to get the ordeal over.
>
> I shuddered when I started on, and decided that the good taste would come afterward. I tried several times more in the course of that long half-mile. Then, astounded by the quantity of beer that was lacking, and remembering having seen stale beer made to foam afresh, I took a stick and stirred what was left till it foamed to the brim.
>
> And my father never noticed. He emptied the pail with the wide thirst of the sweating plowman, returned it to me, and started up the

plow. I endeavored to walk beside the horses. I remember tottering and falling against their heels in front of the shining share, and that my father hauled back on the lines so violently that the horses nearly sat down on me. He told me afterward that it was by only a matter of inches that I escaped disembowelling. Vaguely, too, I remember, my father carried me in his arms to the trees on the edge of the field, while all the world reeled and swung about me and I was aware of deadly nausea mingled with an appalling conviction of sin.

I slept the afternoon away under the trees, and when my father roused me at sundown it was a very sick little boy that got up and dragged wearily homeward. I was exhausted, oppressed by the weight of my limbs, and in my stomach was a harp-like vibration that extended to my throat and brain. My condition was like that of one who had gone through a battle with poison. In truth, I had been poisoned.[18]

In some instances, the outside factor is another person: "I used to stop so my husband wouldn't get mad; I have to go home to my parents, sometimes I'd try to control it to avoid humiliation or blackouts or because of work obligations."

Many nonalcoholics do not enjoy their physical reactions to beverage alcohol. For these persons, there is a disposition to nausea, dizziness and headache after two or three drinks. They become ill very quickly, and will often say that they are drunk on two drinks. I suggest that they have never been drunk. What they are experiencing is a sensitivity to alcohol or its metabolites.

It is very difficult, but not impossible, for persons experiencing these reactions to become alcoholic. I predict that persons whose drinking overrides these physical, adverse, reactions to beverage alcohol due so because of overwhelming personal and cultural pain—what they are seeking is not euphoria so much as anesthesia. We will find these alcoholics primarily among women, the sexually abused, and gays and lesbians. Persons in each of these categories are subject to substantial cultural dissonance and pain that is only faintly understood by those not belonging to these groups. Persons whom we call alcoholics who drink excessive amounts of alcohol in spite of the adverse reactions of oriental flush syndrome are not genetic alcoholics. Their alcoholism is of a different origin, but it is

---

18. London, J. (1981) *John Barleycorn*. Santa Cruz, CA: Western Tanager.

alcoholism nevertheless. Genetic alcoholics exhibit alcoholic behaviors effortlessly. Everybody else has to work hard for their
alcoholism.

*Thus, the first core feature of genetic alcoholism is not the loss of
control, but the lack of it, evidenced from the earliest history of drinking.
It is demonstrated by the lack of a biological satiation response for
beverage alcohol.*

The next core feature is constitutional tolerance for beverage
alcohol. Most people, when they think of tolerance for a drug,
think of acquired tissue tolerance. That is, as a drug is consumed
over time, more and more of it is required to achieve the same
effect. The body chemistry has adapted to the drug. Constitutional
tolerance, on the other hand, is there from the very beginning. It is
not learned. It is biological. Not only that, for our purposes, it is
biologically adaptive.

Let's go back to my first core feature of genetic alcoholism, lack
of satiation. If a person has no satiation for beverage alcohol, no off
switch, sooner or later that person will have unlimited access to
beverage alcohol, together with unlimited reasons for drinking it.
The effect of such combination is a lethal dose of alcohol. In
medicine, a median lethal dose (LD_{50}) of a substance is defined as
the amount of a substance that will kill fifty percent of those
receiving that amount. In medicine, as in everything else, people are
different.[19] With alcohol, LD_{50} usually means a blood alcohol
content of around 0.35 to 0.40.[20] A BAC of 0.35 percent can be
obtained by a 155 pound man consuming 20 ounces of 80 proof
spirits over a two hour period. A woman weighing 110 pounds
reaches this BAC in the same time period by drinking just eleven
and a half ounces of 80 proof spirits.[21]

Death from a lethal dose of alcohol is usually caused by an

19. The correct term is biochemical individuality. See Williams, R. J. (1956)
Biochemical individuality. New York: John Wiley.

20. Cohen, S. (1985) *The substance abuse problems.* (Vol 2) *New issues for the
1980s.* New York: Haworth Press. See also Kinney, J. and Leaton, G. (1987)
Loosening the grip. St. Louis: Times Mirror/Mosby.

21. Alcohol Research Documentation, Inc. (1983). *AlcoCalculator, an educational instrument.* New Brunswick, NJ: Center of Alcohol Studies Rutgers Unver-
sity. This instrument does not tabulate blood alcohol levels in excess of 0.40 percent.

Behavioral Effects of Blood Alcohol Content (B.A.C.) on normal (i.e. non-alcoholic) drinkers[22]	
B.A.C.	**Behavioral Effects**
.05	Diminished alertness, impaired judgement
.10	Slowed reaction time, impaired motor function
.15	Increasingly impaired motor responses
.20	Obvious intoxication
.25	Staggering, grossly impaired motor skills
.30	Stupor, inability to communicate or comprehend one's surroundings
.35	Surgical anesthesia . About LD_1 (the minimal level at which death can occur from overdose).
.40	About LD_{50}
.60	LD_{99} . Just about everybody dies

As Rogers and McMillin observe, the behaviors of alcoholics occur at much greater levels of blood alcohol content than nonalcoholics.

inability to breathe. Listen again to Jack London's story, this time at age 17, having spent the night consuming politicians' free whiskey:

> My sole recollection . . . is of my head out of the window, facing the wind caused by the train, cinders striking and burning and blinding me, while I breathed with will. All my will was concentrated on breathing—on breathing the air in the hugest lung-full gulps I could, pumping the greatest amount of air into my lungs in the shortest possible time. It was that or death, and I was a swimmer and diver and I knew it; and in the most intolerable agony of prolonged suffocation, during those moments I was conscious, I faced the wind and the cinders and breathed for life.[23]

So, if it's true that some people are born with a lack of satiation response to beverage alcohol, then it follows that sooner or later most of them will die from a lethal dose—just drinking too much alcohol in a single drinking episode. Given the early exposure to alcohol in most societies, such persons would probably die before

---

22. Adapted from Rogers, R. L. and McMillin, C. S. (1989). *Don't help*. New York: Bantam.

23. London, J. (1981) *John Barleycorn*. Santa Cruz, CA: Western Tanager.

they had a chance to reproduce their kind. Any of their genes left in the gene pool would be statistically insignificant. Either that, or alcohol would be considered such a toxic poison as to be totally banned for human consumption, in the same manner as lead or lye. Neither of these events has happened.

In the United States, the number of people who die from alcohol overdoses, often in chugalug contests, is so statistically insignificant that it is no longer published as a separate figure.[24] Clearly, the number of persons who die each year from overdoses of beverage alcohol is way out of proportion to the number of people who consume such lethal doses. What's going on here?

In order for a potentially fatal genetic function to survive in such large numbers of people for thousands of years of human development, it must possess a positive attribute that contributes to the survival of the species, or it must be paired with a second gene that modifies the fatal aspects of the first gene.

My imagination cannot come up with any positive reason for a lack of satiation response in humans. I submit for your consideration and investigation, however, that we most often find evidence of *constitutional* tolerance for a lethal dose of alcohol in the same people that have a lack of satiation response for alcohol. We call these people alcoholics.[25]

My own story is somewhat illustrative. On the evening of my eighteenth birthday, then the legal drinking age in New York State, my best friend purchased a case of assorted quarts and fifths of liquor. The idea was that I would drink from each of these bottles in succession, to determine which form of alcohol I liked best, which would from that time on be my best drink. I had been

---

24. U.S. Bureau of the Census. (1990) *Statistical abstract of the United States: 1990*. (110th ed.). Washington, DC. This is not to suggest that the deaths from chug-a-lug contests are in themselves insignificant. On the contrary, they are significant if only because they are entirely avoidable and unnecessary. By statistically insignificant, I mean that the number of deaths from overdoses of alcohol as a percentage of total deaths from alcohol is an extremely low number.

25. One of the mandatory criteria for the diagnosis of alcoholism, according to the National Council on Alcoholism, is a BAC of 0.15 without gross evidence of intoxication. Another is the consumption of a fifth of a gallon of whiskey (or equivalent in beer or wine) on two successive days, by a 180 lb individual. Kissin, B. and Begleiter, H. (1977). *Treatment and rehabilitation of the chronic alcoholic*. New York: Plenum Press.

intoxicated on only one prior occasion. We chose, we thought, a safe place in which to perform this great experiment, an isolated cabin on the Adirondack lake where I grew up. Besides myself and my friend, there were a few other of my high school friends present. That night, I drank my first lethal dose of beverage alcohol. Although there were significant adverse consequences to this episode,[26] I do not remember any significant respiratory distress. It was to prove to be neither my last intoxication, nor my last lethal dose.

Four years later, I was to consume, following a night of drinking, a fifth of corn whiskey in two hours, another lethal dose.

In order for one to become physically addicted to beverage alcohol, one must be able to drink large quantities of it. Some persons are biologically unable to drink large quantities of alcohol, either at one time, or over time, or are biologically not predisposed to do so, because of Oriental Flush, because of satiation, or because alcohol does nothing for them. Others are biologically able to drink large quantities of alcohol, without immediate adverse effect. This is constitutional tolerance.[27]

The second core feature of genetic alcoholism is evidence of constitutional tolerance of beverage alcohol, often marked by the ability to consume a lethal dose of beverage alcohol (LD_{50}).

Goodwin's third core feature, relapse, is the trickiest of all. I suspect that is because it can be separated into several distinct features.

The first is that alcohol (like many other drugs) does something for the alcoholic. Again, in the words of Jack London, "Men do not knowingly drink for the effect alcohol produces on the body. What they drink for is the brain-effect; and if it must come through the body, so much the worse for the body."[28] I think alcoholics drink, and drug addicts take drugs, for only one reason, to get high.[29]

---

26. Thirty years after the event, I am still reminded of it by those who were there.

27. Keller, M., McCormick, M. and Efron, V. (1982). *A dictionary of words about alcohol.* (2nd Ed.). New Brunswick, NJ: Rutgers Center of Alcohol Studies.

28. London, J.(1981) *John Barleycorn.* Santa Cruz, CA: Western Tanager.

29. "High" has many meanings. A good analysis of the word can be found in Cohen, S. (1985). *The substance abuse problems.* (Vol 2.) *New issues for the 1980's.* New York: Haworth Press.

Anything else is just so much illusion and smoke. However we cut it, we drink and do drugs to alter our minds. We express that alteration as a *"higher"* state than before the consumption of alcohol. Again, nonalcoholics are different. Nonalcoholics drink to relax, which is for them a *lower* state than before. Is it possible that both alcoholics and nonalcoholics are trying to reach the same state from different places? Is it possible that alcoholics and nonalcoholics are trying to reach Kansas, the alcoholics from Louisiana, the nonalcoholics from Minnesota?

It's important to listen to the stories of alcoholics for clues as to what is going on.[30] Many alcoholics will tell you that from their very first drink, alcohol was special for them. It was the one substance, and drinking it the one act, that brought mind and body together and made the alcoholic feel integrated and whole. It gave them a sense of well-being. Several things can be deduced from this. One, alcoholics did not feel that way *before* their experience with alcohol. Two, the state they were seeking is disgustingly normal and healthy. It is probably the usual state of most persons outside alcoholic families. If this is true, then it is improper to accuse the alcoholic of being morally degenerate for trying to achieve the same normal state enjoyed by the rest of the population (sometimes referred to by alcoholics as Earth People).

If, prior to the consumption of alcohol, alcoholics do not have a sense of well-being, or of mind/body integration, that can be due to either environmental or genetic factors, or an interaction of both.

Certainly, the child in the environment of an alcoholic family, to a variable, but certain, degree, does not have a sense of well-being. He *and* she are often depressed, anxious about their future and uncomfortable with their present. But this idea of mind–body integration is a very troubling one. It may be what we mean when we say we feel different from other people. At some level of our consciousness, we know that what we feel and what we do not feel is a state that is not shared by others. We spend our lives in a constant search for what other people seem to have. Some of us find alcohol. Others, whose reaction to alcohol is more toxic than that of we alcoholics, very soon find other substances to alter their state:

---

30. George Vaillant recommends that any serious student of alcoholism attend at least 50 meetings of Alcoholics Anonymous. Vaillant, G. (1983). *The natural history of alcoholism*. Cambridge, MA: Harvard University Press. I agree.

food, work, sex, running, stress, danger, and of course, marijuana, cocaine, Valium, heroin, Quaaludes, barbiturates, and the like. And of course, if we stop drinking and do not find natural ways of getting high, we find and pursue those highs that have addictive potential.

These alternative substances and actions have much in common with alcohol. They either mimic neurotransmitters and endorphins or they increase or decrease them. A neurotransmitter is a chemical substance that enables one brain cell (neuron) to communicate with another. Some neurotransmitters are endorphins, a made-up word meaning endogenous (made in the body) morphine. Endorphins are many times more powerful than morphine, have a short half-life, and produce euphoria (make you feel good) just like opium-based drugs such as codeine, morphine, and heroin. The use of alcohol or opiates reduces endorphin producing capacity, which is only slowly restored following the onset of abstinence from those drugs. Exercise, such as running, increases the capacity of the body to make endorphins. Endorphins are also addictive and produce symptoms of withdrawal or discomfort when the activity producing them is discontinued. Moralists should note that endorphins, even though addictive, are no more morally suspect than saliva. They are simply body chemicals that allow us to feel pleasure and ignore pain.[31] As such, they provide the motivation for much of our behavior.

The second part of the relapse factor is the consumption of alcohol despite prior adverse effects, as mentioned in ASAM's definition of alcoholism. This means that learning from experience does not take effect in ways that one would normally expect. For example, during or immediately after a drinking episode, a drinker will experience something unpleasant. Despite the unpleasantness, the person will drink again. During the birthday drinking episode that I related earlier, I wandered outside the cabin in my underwear in extreme below-zero weather, and nearly froze to death. The next day, under the influence of a hangover, I put an axe through a

---

31. The biochemistry of neurotransmitters is explained in a somewhat readable manner in Cohen, S. (1988). *The chemical brain*. Irvine, CA: CareInstitute and in Milkman, H. and Sunderwirth, S. (1987) *Craving for ecstasy*. Lexington, MA: Lexington Books. See also Blum, Kenneth. (1991). *Alcohol and the addictive brain*. New York: Free Press.

brand new boot and sliced a perfectly good foot nearly in two. The following week I got drunk again. Now I'm a college graduate. I even have an advanced degree. I am demonstrably not stupid, retarded or psychotic. I have, on many other occasions, demonstrated that I can, and do, learn from my experience and from the experiences of others. So how come I nearly killed myself, and seven short days later, repeated the same circumstances?

I can only conclude that my memory is selective for euphoria, and not for pain. Recovery from this factor of alcoholism means continually teaching or reminding ourselves that for the alcoholic, the consumption of any amount of alcohol causes pain to ourselves and others in a thousand different ways. We keep our memories green, so to speak, by listening to the accounts of others whose experiences may be similar to ours, usually at AA meetings. We do this for as many times as it takes. Strangely enough, this simple act works, and even more strangely, we derive a fair amount of pleasure from it. The therapy for alcoholism is a lifetime of pleasant experiences gained by talking about our disease with others who are similarly affected. Given these aspects of recovery, and compared to other diseases, alcoholism is a rare and wonderful gift despite the terrible nature of its natural history.

The third core feature of genetic alcoholism is marked by differences in brain function, evidenced by any tendency to relapse, drinking despite adverse consequences, depression in the absence of Central Nervous System depressants, or evidence that the consumption of alcohol performs a significant integrating function.

There's nothing like making something simple without complicating it further. Some of us who have poor impulse control leading to relapse experience impulsivity in the form of a double or triple whammy: first as a core feature of genetic alcoholism, second as a symptom of Attention Deficit Disorder, with or without hyperactivity, and third, as one of the characteristics of the adult child.

Each of these three core features of alcoholism is probably controlled by its own set of genes (multifactorial or polygenic inheritance). The third core feature, relapse, may itself be controlled by several different genes.[32] In addition, some of the genes or gene

---

32. David Rowe notes that, "The family study method can be misinterpreted by scholars lacking an informed understanding of genetic principles. It is often noted that, even when traits run in families, affected children will appear in some families

groups may be sex-limited. Sons of alcoholic fathers become alcoholic, and daughters of alcoholic mothers become alcoholic.

Prediction of who is at risk in any given family to become an alcoholic is very tentative. If an individual shows any evidence of having experienced the behaviors outlined in this chapter, she and he would do well to avoid the consumption of beverage alcohol under any circumstances. The risks are just too high and the rewards too low. If the individual has a desire, given this injunction, not to drink, and still consumes alcohol, it seems to me that this person would be welcome at Alcoholics Anonymous.[33]

If we are to pursue this question of whether or not alcoholism is hereditary, we need to ask, "Why alcohol and not some other beverage?" Why would genes specific to alcohol exist in the first place?[34] A partial answer lies in the metabolism of alcohol. A liver enzyme, alcohol dehydrogenase, changes alcohol to acetaldehyde. Now why an enzyme specific to alcohol? If alcohol is a rather late invention or discovery of man, one would not normally expect to find an enzyme specific to this late invention. Yet, there it is. The reason is that our bodies manufacture approximately an ounce of absolute alcohol per day from intestinal fermentation. The alcohol dehydrogenase begins the metabolic processing of intestinal alcohol as soon as it is formed, with the result that the nondrinker always has a zero blood alcohol content.

Another indicator that alcoholism is or is not genetic in origin is assortative mating, a fancy set of words meaning that like tends to

---

in which neither the mother nor the father is affected. Such results are sometimes misinterpreted as evidence *against* a genetic etiology. To the contrary, whenever a trait is polygenic, new cases often will appear when neither parent is affected, just as a very bright child may be born to parents of average IQ." Rowe, D.C. (1990). Behavior genetic models of alcohol abuse. In Collins, R.L., Leonard, K.E., and Searles, J.S. (Eds.) *Alcohol and the family: research and clinical perspectives.* (107–133) New York: Guilford Press.

33. Tradition Three of Alcoholics Anonymous states that "The only requirement for A.A. membership is a desire to stop drinking." [Wilson, W.G.] (1953). *Twelve steps and twelve traditions.* New York: Alcoholics Anonymous World Services, Inc.

34. This question was asked by Kenneth Weiss to prove that alcoholism could not be genetic in origin. See Weiss, K. (1984). The evolutionary base of alcoholism: a question of the neocortex. In Hartford, J.T. and Samorajski, T. (Eds.). *Alcoholism in the elderly, social and biomedical issues.* New York: Raven Press.

marry like. In other words, when alcoholics tend to marry alcoholics, or when children of alcoholics tend to marry alcoholics, the gene pool is concentrated. The lack of assortative mating is sometimes cited as evidence of that alcoholism is not genetic. Yet, significant numbers of children of alcoholics *do* marry alcoholics. The anecdotal and clinical evidence of assortative mating for alcoholism is substantial, and has even been noted as a characteristic of children of alcoholics.[35] Many children of alcoholics will marry several alcoholics, one after the other. My guesstimate is that probably not more than 50 percent of children of alcoholics marry alcoholics. Yet, this is enough to concentrate substantially the gene pool for alcoholism.

A Suggested Simple Genetic Test for Alcoholism

Satisfy any three of the following four criteria:

1. Lack of satiation for alcohol.
2. (a) Ability to withstand lethal dose, or
   (b) Evidence of high, preaddictive tolerance for alcohol.
3. Evidence of
   (a) failure to learn from alcohol related experience, or,
   (b) history of relapse, or
   (c) evidence that alcohol provides an integrating experience or function.
4. History of alcoholism or other drug addiction in any blood relative, but especially in a blood relative of the same sex.

The earlier any of this evidence occurs in one's drinking and drug history, the more likely are genetic factors to be dominant.

EVIDENCE THAT SATISFIES THE ABOVE CRITERIA

1. Lack of satiation for beverage alcohol.
A. drinking alcohol to intoxication.
B. absence of sensitivity to alcohol, no oriental flush syndrome.
C. external response to drinking cessation.
D. first drink led to first drunk.

---

35. See the Problem and Solution in A., Tony and F., Dan. (1990). *The laundry list: the ACOA experience*. Deerfield Beach, FL: Health Communications.

Questions to ask: During any given drinking episode, why do you (did you) stop drinking once you have started drinking alcohol? Do you stop drinking without a struggle after one or two drinks?[36] Are you always able to stop drinking when you want to?[37] Can you describe the first few times you ever drank alcohol?

Some answers will confuse the interviewer. For example, typical biologically external responses are shared by alcoholics and non-alcoholics alike are those that indicate psychological toxicity to alcohol, otherwise known to the psychiatric profession as reaction formation: fear of being an alcoholic like a parent or husband, fear of being labeled a drunk, aware that they're at risk for alcoholism because of family or personal history.

2. Lethal dose and High tolerance.
A. Anecdotal experience of tolerance.
B. Pride in tolerance.
C. Evidence of physical addiction.
D. Binge drinking.
E. BAC at any time over 0.3.

Questions to ask: What's the most you have ever had to drink at one time? Over how long a time period was that? Did you ever have difficulty in breathing before you passed out? Can you drink more than your peers? What's the worst drinking episode you ever had? How long ago was that?

If there is no evidence of tolerance for alcohol, and evidence of lack of satiation response, and/or any criteria for relapse occur, then the patient *must* be warned that he/she is at extraordinary risk from early death from alcohol intoxication because there are no natural or genetic controls to act as a barrier to consuming too much alcohol.

3. Relapse
A. Drinking again after prior bad experience with alcohol.
B. On again, off again drinking behavior.

---

36. Modified from Question #4 of the Michigan Alcoholism Screening Test (MAST).

37. Question #8 from MAST.

C. Second intoxication on heels of first intoxication.
D. Evidence that alcohol provides integration.
E. Driving while intoxicated after having been arrested for the same offense.
F. Evidence that consumption of 100 percent RDA of Vitamin B6, either alone or in combination with other vitamins, minerals, and amino acids is an effective preventer of relapse where relapse has been previously demonstrated.[38]
G. Continuing need to get high.

Questions to ask: What does (did) alcohol do for you? What was your first drinking experience like? Did you get drunk? What happened? When did you drink again? What happened then? Have you ever been told by a doctor to stop drinking? Have you ever stopped drinking and then started again? How many times? Has drinking ever created problems with your spouse? (or children?; or parents?; or school?; or job?) How much coffee do you drink during the day?[39] Is this decaf or regular? What is your sugar consumption like?

4. Family history of alcoholism.
A. Any blood relative with a history of alcohol related problems.[40]
B. If the client is adopted, assume that a biological parent is alcoholic. This is a fair assumption if the over-consumption of alcohol is present during most instances of first and early sexual

---

38. According to Carl Pfeiffer, Vitamin B6 deficiency can be diagnosed by evidence of lack of dreaming. Pfeiffer, C. (1987). *Nutrition and mental illness an orthomolecular approach to nalancing body chemistry.* Rochester, VT: Healing Arts. The proof is that vitamin B6 restores REM sleep, and thus restores dreaming. I told one physician this and he practically accused me of practicing medicine without a license. He took the vitamins to prove me wrong, and he's still taking them ten years later.

39. This and the following questions determine the extent of lifestyle consumption of diuretics which deplete the body of water soluble vitamins such as vitamin C and the B vitamins. See the chapter on Living With Chronic Depression.

40. Criteria for a history of alcoholism in any relative are less vigorous than those for yourself. See Andreason, N. C., Endicott, J., Spitzer, R.L., and Winokur, G.L. (1977). The family history method using diagnostic criteria. *Archives of General Psychiatry. 34,* 1229-1235.

intercourse. The offspring of such encounters are more likely to be adopted.[41]

Persons who respond positively only to the third criteria, relapse, are perhaps more likely to be users of drugs other than alcohol or to experience symptoms of depression.

No diagnosis of alcoholism is useful unless that diagnosis is successfully conveyed to the patient. No diagnosis can be successfully conveyed if it is accompanied by shame or blame. If the diagnosis is accompanied by shame or blame, the alcoholic will deny the diagnosis and continue drinking. Two hundred years ago, Dr. Benjamin Rush, the first American to call alcoholism a disease, called upon preachers to denounce the seducing influence of toddy and grog, and suggested that shame and guilt be used to prevent the recurrence of fits of drunkenness.[42] Rush's opinion as a physician was perhaps influenced by his stepfather Richard Morris, a "rough, unkind and often abusive" distiller.[43] Unfortunately, Rush's work had a greater influence on the preaching community than on the medical community. The preachers like Lyman Beecher picked up the banner of shame and guilt and made drunkenness a sin.[44] Organized religion thus unwittingly contributed indirectly to the perpetuation of active alcoholism in untold millions of alcoholics. It's time to bring this process to a screeching halt by recognizing that alcoholics are not responsible for acquiring their disease. They are responsible only for their behaviors during the course of the disease, and for treating it. Their acquisition of alcoholism was no more willful than their acquisition of any other disease.

---

41. Your average adolescent may not know that Ogden Nash said it first, but he does know from his own and peer experience that "candy is dandy, but liquor is quicker."

42. Rush, B. (c1784). *An inquiry into the effects of ardent spirits upon the human mind and body*. Philadelphia: Thos Bradford.

43. Corner, G.W. (Ed.). (1948). *The autobiography of Benjamin Rush*. Princeton: Princeton University Press.

44. Beecher, Lyman. (1827). *Six sermons on the nature, occasions, signs, evils, and remedy of intemperance*. New York: American Tract Society. The influence of Rush on the formation of the first temperance society and upon Lyman Beecher is noted in Cherrington, E.H. (1929) *Standard Encyclopedia of the Alcohol Problem*. (Vol V) Westerville, OH: American Issue Publishing Company.

6 ...

Living with Chronic Depression

I hadn't been sober in my recovery very long when I discovered that I had been depressed. I had been down so far for so long the depths in which I lived were the only home I knew. It wasn't until I had some experience of not being depressed that I understood how low I had been. I quickly learned that I could experience repetitive natural highs simply by going to meetings where people talked about their use and abuse of alcohol.

I was one of the so-called high bottom drunks, who enrolled in a recovery program not so much because I had hit bottom, but because I had had the good fortune to be the child of a recovering alcoholic who was also an alcoholism counselor. Visiting Mom was a little bit like visiting a rehab. Every time I visited, I got a little more education. So I went to meetings, not because I didn't want to drink anymore, but because I didn't want to be an alcoholic. I continued to attend because I discovered a way to get high without a hangover.

In spite of being sober, however, I continued to get depressed. Conventional wisdom at the time had it that all I had to do to get rid of my depression was (a) to stop drinking and (b) to get rid of my "internalized" anger. After four years of sobriety and three years of therapy, I still got depressed. However, I became quite skillful in getting rid of the depression. I learned that any motion, no matter how directionless, was better than no motion at all. I learned to vocalize my feelings—usually of rage—and dump on a disinterested third party, my-self help group sponsor. I made attempts at becoming assertive and my attempts worked. I went back to graduate school, using the energy wrapped up in my anger to save the world from alcoholism. I found a different self-help group and learned that I no longer needed to feel or to act responsible for my actively alcoholic relatives. My feelings of helplessness disappeared when I learned to separate my problems from the problems of others and to take responsibility only for what was truly my own. Blessed relief! The war in Afghanistan was no longer my problem. But still, I got depressed.

I took comfort in the idea that my depressions, which in my drinking days had lasted months, now only lasted days or weeks. I had become familiar and comfortable with the routine cycle of intermittent highs and lows of my moods. I learned through photographs of myself as a child that I had been depressed all through childhood. Pictures of a young and smiling Tom are rare. As a recovering adult, I still didn't smile much, but I no longer shuffled my feet when I walked. Relative to those pits, I was high all the time. My lows never reached the depths that I once called home.

Shortly after I began holding workshops for adult children of alcoholics, it became evident to me that adult children had poor eating habits. Studies on eating disorders showed that significant numbers of that population were children of the chemically dependent. Our workshop participants reported that their childhood breakfasts often consisted of cold pizza and Coke. Dinners came out of a can and often the same meal was repeated night after night. Children of alcoholics with absentee parents ate what they could forage, overeating when there was plenty and learning to make do with little or none when that was the condition. Others were survivors of having been sexually abused as children, and overate so that their fathers or uncles would think them fat and ugly. (It didn't work. They became fat, but the sexual abuse continued nevertheless.)

Many physicians assume that most people get a perfectly adequate supply of vitamins from the food they eat. They dismiss the taking of vitamin supplements by saying that Americans have the most expensive urine in the world. It is prudent to test such assumptions before announcing them as fact, especially if you slept through the one hour of nutritional instruction you received during your years in medical school.[1]

It is relatively easy to test whether or not your diet is adequate. Keep a daily diary of what you eat, recording both the type and amounts of food consumed during each meal or snack. Use a food scale to weigh your food portions. Look up the vitamin content in the book *Food Values of Portions Commonly Used*[2] for each entry in your diary. Do this daily for two weeks to determine your average daily vitamin intake.

As a recovering bachelor adult, my diet was hardly nutritious. A sample daily diet went something like this:

Breakfast	2 cups coffee, no milk, no sugar
	2 plain doughnuts
Break	2 cups coffee, no milk, no sugar
Lunch	2 cups coffee, no milk, no sugar
	2 slices pizza, Diet Coke
Break	2 cups coffee, no milk, no sugar
Supper	1 glass whole milk
	2 cheeseburgers
	1 order French fries (3 oz.)
Meeting	2 cups coffee, no milk, no sugar

My point is that nutritional consumption varies widely from day to day, from meal to meal. One day, the vitamin content may be sufficient, the next day it is not. On the whole, my guess is that adequate nutrition is a sometime thing for most of the population with which I am concerned: alcoholics, their spouses, and their offspring. If it happens, it happens by chance rather than by design.

With this background, I became interested in the idea of introducing nutritional material into our workshops, with the result that I became involved, somewhat naively, in the consumption of moderately heavy doses of vitamins.

Bear in mind that I, in addition to being the child of an alcoholic,

---

1. Physicians commonly do not learn much, if anything, about sex, human relationships, counseling, hypnosis, nutrition, or alcoholism in medical school. It's probably human nature to ridicule things about which you are ignorant, but in these instances, the ignorance has tragic consequences.

2. Pennington, J. A. T. (1989). *Food values of portions commonly used*. New York: Harper & Row.

am also the child of a drug addict. I was then, and remain today, disdainful of any drug not in liquid form. But vitamins were harmless, I was told. Any excess I didn't need would be flushed away, with the remainder to be used by various parts of the body as may be appropriate. So I purchased a thirty-day supply of a multiple vitamin and consumed them all on schedule.

Two things happened. One, I did not get depressed for thirty consecutive days. For the first time in my remembered life I experienced a month, not of highs and lows, but of flat norms. I had my successes in that month, and my failures. An event that would once have kept me giddy for a month kept me well pleased for three days. A curt and unfair criticism that would have had me mumbling under my breath for days was received as if it had not been received at all. Going for thirty days of normal was like spending thirty days in San Francisco after forty years in Siberia. The second happening was that my supply of vitamins became exhausted, and being cheap, I purchased no more. Obviously, vitamins were not addictive.

A few months later, coming home from the movies, my car rebelled against years of neglect and overuse. The bill for repair and temporary replacement came to $1,200 that I didn't have. That's depressing, and appropriately, I got depressed. When after I had done all the things I had learned to do to get undepressed, and I was still depressed, I tried a multiple vitamin borrowed from a friend. The result was that I was back on that flat norm. I was no longer crushed and I could deal rationally with my situation.

I spent the summer going through on-again, off-again[3] situations with vitamins, trying various combinations and strengths. I found that megadoses of the B-vitamins gave me arthritic-like pains, and I dropped the idea of megadoses. Being thirty-nine was bad enough without artificially induced arthritis. The daily newspaper reported that megadoses of some vitamins would produce nerve damage. So much for the harmless. Could my obsessive/compulsive ego find true happiness in being moderate? Eventually, I found several manufacturers who marketed a combination pill with only the Recommended Dietary Allowance (RDA) of each vitamin. This seemed to work just fine.

---

3. In the academic world, this is called single case research design, and is just as valid as any other controlled study.

So much for the story. What's the theory behind it? Why should vitamins work so well with my depression? I had neither bio-chemical nor nutritional training to help me understand what was going on in my mind and body. Was my experience a random event? Would my vitamins have the same effect on others.

I started looking at my life-style and those of my clients. Hope-lessly addicted to coffee, I was drinking twenty-some odd cups of coffee a day. Although I had not had a drink in over nine years, I would go on binges of chocolate bars/cake/cookies/ice cream. I hadn't smoked in over ten years, but my clients very often were consuming some two or three packs of cigarettes daily. A little research indicated that my clients and I were consuming impressive quantities of natural diuretics. Our consumption of caffeine, sugar, and alcohol, all diuretics, was causing us rapid loss of the water soluble vitamins.[4] A little more research showed that the water-soluble B-vitamins were those most important for brain function, especially Thiamine, Niacin, and B6. A chance reading of an article in our health food store reported that one characteristic of vitamin B6 deficiency was the absence of dreams other than nightmares. I thought of the three years in therapy I had spent trying to come up with dreams for my psychodynamically trained therapist. Some of my acquaintances reported that in similar situations they had even invented dreams in an attempt to convince their therapists that they weren't being resistant. One day's regimen of a B-vitamin supple-ment and no coffee produced a plethora of easily remembered deep sleep dreams.

As a result of personal and clinical experience over the last decade, I have formed the following hypotheses:

Alcoholics and children of alcoholics are often deficient in B-vitamins. Their deficiency results *primarily* from the overconsump-tion of agents (sugar, caffeine, alcohol) originally consumed to alter mood (i.e., get high, relax) and from the poor nutritional habits picked up in childhood. In addition, there may be some dysfunc-tion in the manufacture of neurotransmitters from B6 and amino

---

4. Potent diuretics, in the presence of muscle relaxants, central nervous system depressants, digitalis, and antibiotics such as Neomycin are potentially fatal. Source: Martin, E. W. (1978). *Hazards of medication*. Philadelphia: Lippincott. Prozac®, this year's magic bullet, is a powerful diuretic. As such, it leaves much to be desired.

acids. Alcoholics recovering in Alcoholics Anonymous continue to try to regulate their mood through the overconsumption of caffeine and sugar. As an unconscious attempt to medicate themselves against Attention Deficit Disorder with Hyperactivity, they use caffeine to relax.[5] Coffee is a socially acceptable amphetaminelike central nervous system stimulant, which may have the same paradoxical calming effect that Ritalin has on ADHD sufferers. The price of the relaxing effect is the diuretic effect, which in conjunction with poor eating habits learned in childhood or acquired during late stages of alcoholism, combine with other properties of these agents into self-destructive cycles.

These vitamin deficiencies, in their early stages, are characterized by apathy and depression. In addition, caffeine, by stimulating the release of glycogen from the liver), alcohol and sugar itself, aggravate hypoglycemia, a depressive reaction from the overproduction of insulin thought to be found in most alcoholics.

The vitamin deficiencies acquired by the mechanisms outlined above may aggravate a hypothetical preexisting biogenetic defect (hereditary depression), which in turn, could conceivably result from a diminished ability to utilize one or more vitamins or amino acids.

The diminished ability to metabolize one or more vitamins or amino acids, especially vitamin B6, plays a role in the lack of production of neurotransmitters. One interesting clue for this is that a vitamin B6 dependency has been induced in normal adults given a supplement of 200 mg. of pyrodoxine (one of the ingredients of B6) daily for thirty-three days while they were ingesting a normal diet. The recommended daily dose for adults is 2.2 mg for males and 2.0 for females.[6]

One way to test this theory would be to compare the amounts of

---

5. Ritalin (methylphenidate hydrochloride), a central nervous system stimulant less powerful than amphetamine, but stronger than caffeine, is usually prescribed for ADHD. Many recovering alcoholics are also addicted to amphetamines. As such, abstinence from amphetamines and amphetaminelike stimulants is as required for sobriety as is abstinence from alcohol. Coffee has always been a major feature at AA meetings. Alcoholics Anonymous always notes with pride the enormous quantities of coffee consumed at its conventions held every five years.

6. National Academy of Sciences. (1980). *Recommended dietary allowances*. (9th ed.). Washington, D.C.: National Academy Press.

the neurotransmitters beta-endorphins and serotonin in the cere-brospinal fluid of nonalcohol-using children of alcoholics with children with no history of familial alcoholism, with alcoholics who have a history of continuous sobriety, and with active alcoholics. Since obtaining cerebrospinal fluid is a dangerous and painful process, it would be unethical to test individuals solely for the purposes of such an experiment. However, fluid obtained for other legitimate medical purposes would serve just as well.

In the absence of funds to develop and test my theories, I use the following regimen as a prophylactic and treatment for depression in adult children of alcoholics and for alcoholic relapse.

1. Regular and frequent attendance at meetings of Alcoholics Anonymous and such other self-help groups as may be appropriate. Inherent in this recommendation is the acquisition of a personal support system consisting of interpersonal relationships of varying intimacy.

2. Elimination of alcohol, nicotine, caffeine, sugar, and refined carbohydrates (white flour, white sugar, and white rice) from the diet. Sugar should not be eliminated until after the client has completely withdrawn from alcohol or five days after the last drink, whichever is later. This will help prevent glucose shock and perhaps seizures and the DTs. The immediate cessation of smoking during early sobriety runs counter to the folk wisdom of AA and most alcoholism rehabilitation units, although that is now changing somewhat. A holistic approach to recovery takes note of the dangers of nicotine and its role in self-destructive cycles of behavior. A corollary of this recommendation is that the nonsmoking, co-dependent alcoholism counselor no longer tolerates smoking during a session because he/she wants to be liked by the client. Another corollary is that the alcoholism counselor must deal with nicotine addiction in the same manner and with the same degree of forcefulness as that of any other drug addiction. In other words, the nicotine addicted counselor is *not* an appropriate role model for the recovering alcohol addict. If caffeine continues to be chosen for its relaxing effects, the client needs to be made aware that the price of caffeine is a daily supplement of vitamins.

Withdrawal from caffeine takes about five days. It can be accomplished relatively painlessly by abstaining from coffee until the headache inevitably appears, then taking one half cup of regular coffee. Subsequent headaches, which are resistant to aspirin and acetaminophen (Tylenol), should appear at increasingly greater intervals until total withdrawal is accomplished. Consumption of chocolate, (containing 15g caffeine per ounce), decaffeinated coffee (2–3g per ounce), and caffeine-containing colas (35–50g per ounce), are sufficient to reactivate the addiction. Withdrawal from caffeine promotes better sleep and, in the absence of alcohol, eliminates morning hangovers.

Recovering alcoholics and their families would do well to recognize their continuing need to regulate mood. Substitutes for both caffeine and sugar can be offered, and the original drugs eliminated from meetings. Protein snacks at meetings would be a welcome and therapeutic addition. Before we had effective professional treatment for alcoholics, the sugar available at AA meetings was probably quite instrumental in preventing glucose shock from the too rapid withdrawal from the sugar in alcohol. Now that many newcomers to AA come directly from hospitals or whose addiction is less advanced, the possible preventative effects of caffeine and sugar are outweighed by their contribution to depression and to relapse.

3. Use of a daily multi-vitamin with minerals, equivalent to *Theragram M with Zinc* for the first ninety days of sobriety/treatment followed by the equivalent of Schiff's *ALL RDA*. Alternatively, the SAAVE™ product, consisting of the amino acids L-glutamine, Dl-phenylalanine, and several vitamins and minerals, is often prescribed for relapse-prone alcohol addicts.[7] I am personally impressed with the effects of the milder EAASE™ on my own chronic depression. EAASE™ is a formulation similar to SAAVE™, and made for the stress-prone individual. None of these formulations make one high or alter mood in the fashion of chemicals of abuse. What they do is provide the body with the building blocks of neurotransmitters. The body then makes whatever neurotransmitters it needs, in the amount that it needs, and discards what it does not need.

4. Daily aerobic exercise lasting from fifteen minutes to one hour. Among other reasons for the promotion of exercise, it stimulates neurotransmitter production. I usually suggest vigorous walking in a safe neighborhood as opposed to running or a health club. For

---

7. Distributed by Matrix Technologies, Houston, TX.

married clients, or those in a loving relationship, I strongly suggest that the client invite his/her partner, and hold hands during the walk. This ritual provides a climate where intimacy and love can flourish. Running tends to be addictive (perhaps due to excessive endorphin production), hurts the feet and decreases the potential for intimacy just when intimacy is most needed.

5. Three to four small balanced meals daily. The alcoholic's norm of skipping breakfast aggravates hypoglycemia. A regular breakfast of complex carbohydrates helps prevent hypoglycemia induced bingeing/overeating.

Does this work, or is this just another fruitless search for an easier, softer way to recover?

An alcoholic client referred for counseling because of several relapses while attending AA helped shed some light on the nature of depressions and what I have come to call, in polite society, "The Hell with It" syndrome. John had relapsed to drinking after more than twelve months of continuous sobriety, and then came to counselling. A week after his first counselling session, John got drunk again, totaled his new car, and was left by his wife. The day he drank, John, who was an avid fisherman, had gone deep sea fishing. Several miles off the coast, the boat broke down and no fishing could be attempted. John said, "The hell with it," and accepted a beer from the other disappointed fisherman on board, with the results stated above.

The experience of John's sudden loss and consequent depression was sufficient to send him below a threshold of vulnerability, from which his only known recourse was alcohol.

During the 1981 workshop on Women in Crisis in New York City, Dr. Stanley Gitlow of the Mt. Sinai School of Medicine suggested that being with, and talking to, other persons at an emotional level who were similarly affected had an elevating effect on one's endorphin level with a consequent rise in one's mood. Among the evidence he cited was the extraordinary overlap among membership in the various self-help groups. Endorphins (endogenous morphine) are naturally occurring opiatelike peptides found in the brain and the pituitary. They are thirty times more powerful than morphine, are metabolized in about four hours; their production is inhibited by the consumption of alcohol and increased by stress and exercise. It should be remembered that Alcoholics Anonymous began when Bill Wilson discovered that he no longer felt like drinking when he was talking with another alcoholic.

I wondered whether John's threshold of vulnerability was all the more precarious because he was without AA companions on the boat. We tested Gitlow's theory by having John chart his mood swings during the day. When John was working with other people, he was up. When he was eating lunch alone, he was down. Moods tended to be elevated when he was in the company of other people, and down when he was alone. Thus, Gitlow's theory had some practical application.

The implication for the adult child of the alcoholic parent, who shares a common genetic background with the parent, is especially important. Many adult children have learned, like myself, to become professional loners. Most of us have characteristics of the lost child within us. If Gitlow's theory that being with other people increases our endorphin levels holds up, it would provide a potent rationale for continuing attendance at AA meetings. One meeting is not enough, for the endorphins (and consequent feelings of well-being) produced by the endorphins disappear during the four hours following the meeting.

Gitlow's theory also suggests why membership in peer groups is so powerful. If one's neurotransmitters are continually elevated by being among one's friends in a pub or other peer group, it will be very difficult to persuade one to leave such a group, no matter how dysfunctional it may be for him.

7   •••

So What?

A friend of mine, sober in AA for many years, once suggested to me with more than a little seriousness that we start a movement to stamp out the search for the root causes of alcoholism. His belief was that (a) we had the disease, (b) we had found a method to arrest it, and (c) that our recovery and our lives depended on using that method. If we got sidetracked from our primary purpose, we endangered our recovery.

I continue to be amazed by the number of researchers who forgot or never knew the history of addictions. Researchers who continue to search for and prescribe new drugs as a cure for the addictive properties of old drugs, which in turn were originally created to cure still another addiction never seem to learn from the experience of others. My friend's point is well taken.

Nevertheless, there are some interesting and profound implications for all of us if alcoholism is, in fact, hereditary.

Genetic diseases are, by definition, chronic, progressive, incurable and often fatal. That definition sounds suspiciously similar to the description of alcoholism used by self-help groups over the last fifty years.

If alcoholism is a genetic disease, then by definition alcoholism is uncontrollable. Expenditures of time, money and energy for controlling the alcoholic's personal consumption of alcoholic beverages is time, money and energy wasted. Again, this sounds unsurprisingly similar to what Alchoholics Anonymous has been telling us all these years.

To put it another way: Anheuser-Busch has a campaign on college campuses that advertises the need for young people to learn to drink responsibly. If alcoholism is a genetic disease, the type of which I have described here, some ten to twenty percent of the student population will never learn to drink responsibly.[1] They can't learn, because their primary response to beverage alcohol is a physical response, not a thinking response. If a person needs to control his or her drinking, the drinking is already out of control. That is a genetic problem, rather than a moral indictment or a learning problem.

For fathers[2] who want to teach their children how to drink at an early age by giving them wine at the dinner table, the response will be equally futile. The quantity of the beverage may well be controlled by the parent, but for those who are genetically alcoholic, the satiation response will remain unquenched. I will never forget my seven-year-old brother, as alcoholic as I, who, upon being poured two fingers of wine in a tumbler at dinner, cried out "Bien plus que ça!" (A lot more than that!).

If alcoholism is a genetic disease, then most of the preaching for the last two hundred years has been based on false premises, and is therefore, very wrong. As I write this, there is an evangelical minister (Josh McDowell) on the radio telling his audience that alcohol and drug abuse are not problems, but are symptoms of a greater problem. The winds of change are upon us, however. My bookstores, which specialize in alcoholism, among other things, cater to increasing numbers of fundamentalist and other Protestant ministers, Franciscan Friars, Dominican nuns, Roman Catholic priests, and rabbis, all sincere women and men of faith. A Baptist minister, Donald Tumblin, has developed a drug and alcohol curriculum for Southern Baptist Churches that goes a long way toward redressing centuries of misinformation.[3] Matthew Fox has written

---

1. George Gallup reports that 17 per cent of seniors at an Ivy League University admitted to having a drinking problem. Gallup, G., Jr. (1987). *Alcohol Use and Abuse in America*. Gallup Report No. 265. October, 1987. Princeton, NJ: The Gallup Organization.

2. I suspect that mothers know better without being told this.

3. Tumblin, D.C. *The Development of an Alcohol and Drug Educational Curriculum for Southern Baptist Churches*. Unpublished doctoral dissertation. Atlanta: Erskine Theological Seminary, 1988.

the Catholic Church an open letter inviting it to examine itself as a dysfunctional and co-dependent family.

Alcoholism was never a symptom, and never a sin, any more than our enabling of it was. The things our parents did to us were unthinking reactions to a disease they never knew they had.

While the drinking of alcohol is hardly a moral question, the public promotion of alcohol consumption to the group at highest risk for inheriting the disease, may, indeed, be morally and ethically questionable. If the alcohol industry is to profit from capturing drinkers at an early age, and turning them into active alcoholics, then it should be required, at the very least, to fund prevention advertising in equal amounts, with the control of such funds being placed outside their hands. Since the greatest environmental precursor of alcoholism is other drug use by parents (i.e. smoking), then a similar argument can be made for the funding of smoking-prevention advertisements by the tobacco industry. In other words, I am not opposed to the advertising of tobacco and alcohol by the consumption interests. I just want equal time for an opposing message to be funded by the same interests.

If alcoholism is a genetic disease, children who are at risk for alcoholism are also at risk for being labeled and being discriminated against. Minor children, and those adults who have not yet recovered from either their own alcoholism or parental alcoholism, are at grave risk for being singled out by the media, and exploited for the emotional and sensational content of their stories. These persons are unable to provide informed consent, and their right to keep their names and faces anonymous should always be protected. Society needs to require ethical safeguards to prevent such exploitation by the media.

The greater the public knowledge of alcoholism and its effects on the family, the greater the consequences for those who seek public office. The ACOA who runs for political office would have the unfair burden of establishing that she or he has recovered from all of parental alcoholism's side effects.

But probably the greatest benefit of alcoholism's being a genetic disease is that primary prevention becomes a real possibility, at least every other generation. For almost two decades, we have seen the sons and daughters of recovering alcoholics enter treatment in their teens and early twenties. The children with whom I got sober in the midseventies are now in their thirties, never having consumed a legal alcoholic beverage. The first and second generation sobriety of parents and grandparents has given the third generation a headstart on avoiding family dysfunction.

If the diagnostic criteria I have outlined in this book become accepted and a part of common knowledge, then children and those around them will be able to diagnose their alcoholism as early as their second intoxication. By then, the pattern of genetic alcoholism will have begun to emerge. At this stage, there is little psychological attachment to alcohol, and the achievement of abstinence is less of a conflict than at any other time in life. If alcoholism is as common as the common cold, then perhaps its symptoms will be equally recognized. But unlike the common cold virus, alcoholism does not mutate.[4] However, some children of each generation will forget or not know that their parents or grandparents were actively alcoholic. But if the community that surrounds them understands the earliest of symptoms of genetic alcoholism, then perhaps our social mores with regard to alcohol might more likely approach those of Jews who stay close to their religion and to their community. Although alcohol may be prized among religious Jews, drunkenness is not. The Jew who exhibits a lack of satiation response to alcohol is told, very quickly, by his family and his community that he drinks like the *goyim*, like *them*, and that it would be better for him that he not drink at all.

What this means is that the person who is intoxicated is at grave risk for *being*, not becoming, an alcoholic. Intoxication is a primary symptom of genetic alcoholism. Intoxication is primary evidence of lack of control. If alcoholism is under genetic control, one is, or is not, an alcoholic. One does not become alcoholic.

Let me illustrate this with another story. I once had lunch with a physician who, during the course of the meal, stated that she had a patient who was about to become an alcoholic. Of course this remarkable statement piqued my interest, and I wondered out loud how she knew of his approaching alcoholism. Her reply was that

---

4. It can be argued that the search for new and more exotic mind-altering drugs or the search for chemical cures for alcoholism, which invariably turn out to be as addictive as the substances they were designed to cure, is a form of mutation. It's very sad that persons involved with drug and alcohol abuse seem destined to repeat the lessons of history.

her patient was about to go into Delirium Tremens.[5] My angry response was that her diagnosis was the same as diagnosing pregnancy when the mother is about ready to go into labor.

To take my analogy even further, I look forward to the day when alcoholism is as easily diagnosed by the layperson as is pregnancy. There will always be a need for sophisticated tests for early diagnosis that remain the province of the clinician. But if my five-year old can make an educated guess of pregnancy at six months, then the same child observing the symptoms of alcoholism early in the course of the disease should be able to make a fairly educated guess that alcoholism is present. And if he can make such a diagnosis in others, he may be able to make it in himself should the opportunity arise.

---

5. Another sad part about this exchange was that our physician was apparently unaware that Delirum Tremens is largely preventable in a treatment setting.

8   ...

Who's on First, What's on Second?

Several years ago, I received an inquiry from a school psychology student in Idaho about treatment strategies for substance abuse. My response, which follows, draws on my own experience in recovery and in my treatment of alcoholic families.

Writing this response gave me the opportunity to think out what had been a loose collection of operating principles for the treatment of alcoholics and their family members. What follows is a formula for the treatment of alcoholism, substance abuse, sedativism, chemical dependency, co-dependency, or, for that matter, any other life-threatening dependency. This is a macroformula, a linking and ordering of experiences. I suspect that this formula will hold true for just about any school of therapy.

The formula consists of a series of assumptions that form the basis of my substance abuse treatment. These are not self-evident truths; I learned each of them the hard way, through trial and error. I have found that whenever I neglect these assumptions or forget them, I risk hurting my client and delay the healing process.

Any technique or style that respects the client's dignity will offer considerable assurance of success. Therapies or groups destructive for children of alcoholics or for any client are those that in any way and as part of their program would deprive a person of basic bodily needs (sleep, food, elimination, etc.) in order to achieve some psychological goal. Children of alcoholics and alcoholics benefit from avoiding persons in authority who are coercive, threatening, controlling, demeaning, humiliating or in any other way abusive.

The first essential concept in the treatment of chemical dependency is the understanding and acceptance by the therapist that the client's continued use of mood-altering chemicals confounds therapy and has multiple, long-term toxic effects on the user's central nervous system.

I am constantly reminded that alcohol is a toxin, as are marijuana and the tranquilizers. Controlled use of toxins only means that the damage done by the toxins occurs more slowly than by uncontrolled use. The damage still occurs. The time that could have been devoted to recovery is still lost. Even small amounts of alcohol and other mood-altering drugs will have a detrimental effect on the course of therapy. The reason is that the client learns that feelings can be medicated, suppressed, or avoided by chemicals. Since the primary therapeutic mechanism is to regain access to one's feelings, the use of such mood-altering substances confounds the recovery process. In addition, the client's family adopts a repertoire of survival techniques that become increasingly inappropriate and harmful as the use of chemicals progresses. If the client's continued use of chemicals is condoned by the therapist, the recovery of the client's family becomes problematic.

Therapists who condone controlled use of alcohol in their clients should do so only if they wish to enrich themselves at the expense of their clients. This process probably will not end until recovering clients begin to recover damages from their therapists through litigation.

The next assumption involves my attitude toward my client. My client is my client, and not my patient, partly because I do not often see sick people, but mostly because I do not play doctor. People who are sick need medical treatment and I am not a physician. The use of the word *patient* to refer to persons who are not being seen by a medical doctor and who are not institutionalized seems to me to be a bit pretentious. The person whose body has not yet detoxified from chemicals may be sick. Indeed, she may be, and often is, deathly ill from the continued effects of alcohol and other drugs. But when the client has been detoxified, or has never used alcohol or other mood changing drugs, I do the individual a disservice if I encourage him to use a word that society uses to demean people.

Implicit in this assumption is the idea that my client is fundamentally healthy and capable of growth. It is axiomatic in family therapy that the therapist usually works with the healthiest member of the family.[1] By my adoption of this attitude, I reinforce and promote wellness and growth rather than their opposites. Many of us who grow up in alcoholic families have a fear of being thought insane, for to be insane is to be thought in some way inadequate. It is only later, in the advanced stages of alcoholism, that we prefer insanity to giving up the booze.

My client may be confused, distraught, torn and hurting. He may also be rigid, inconsistent and manipulative. The source of these difficulties lies not in sickness or pathology as much as in isolation and ignorance.

Ignorance is not a character defect: it is simply a lack of information. The client lacks information because (a) the problem of chemical dependency is complex, (b) we haven't discovered all the answers yet, and (c) nobody educated the client. Isolation and ignorance are progressive and feed on each other, producing a host of behaviors in user and family members that appear to be pathological.

Simply and elegantly, the treatment for chemical dependency is to educate, in the company of others, those affected by it. Education, in its simplest form, means filling the data banks that were previously empty. It also means resorting or rearranging the data already present so that patterns previously unnoticed may be unrecognized. Once patterns are recognized, the client's energies can be focused on dealing with the pattern rather than being spread over a number of apparently random events. This is not to say that we do not need therapy. Our wounds are deep, the scars we bear are often crippling, and they need healing.

Those affected by alcohol include, but are not limited to, the person who is chemically dependent, his/her family, employers, schools, and the community as a whole. Although the chemically dependent person constitutes a minority in our society, he sets the

---

1. Since there are more women in therapy than men, and since more women buy and read growth books than men, I can only conclude that women in our society are fundamentally healthier than men. Men, on the other hand, buy bumper stickers, and read them. Perhaps the men's movement will change this.

norm for all of us. One goal of treatment is to reverse that process.

Group treatment is the best option because it is (a) cheaper, (b) more therapeutic, (c) quicker, and (d) reaches more people. Circles of active clients are more efficient than rows of passive subjects, which means that a group dynamics orientation has better results than the traditional classroom approach.

The search to find and describe the alcoholic personality is a fool's errand. The alcoholic personality as such does not exist. What many persons refer to as the alcoholic personality may be that set of behaviors that children of alcoholics adopt to survive in their family of origin. Other aspects of the so-called alcoholic personality are to be found in symptoms of Attention Deficit Disorder. No personality type is immune from alcoholism and other forms of chemical dependency. When these children or grandchildren of alcoholics grow older and adopt the use of alcohol and other drugs, the chemicals exaggerate the characteristics of personality formed in infancy and childhood.

The use of mood-altering chemicals also retards emotional development. Thus, our chemically dependent clients are emotionally immature, a condition that will persist indefinitely if the use of chemicals by the client also continues. That alone should be sufficient to dissuade helpers from trying to control the drinking of alcoholics.

The hierarchy of treatment preference for any person affected by chemical dependency begins with multiple-family treatment and continues through single family treatment, peer group treatment (self-help or professionally led),[2] individual treatment with a person trained in chemical dependency, no treatment, and lastly, individual treatment with a person not trained in chemical dependency.

This last statement warrants emphasizing. *No treatment at all is preferable to so-called treatment by persons who are ignorant of chemical dependency dynamics and treatment methods.* No treatment is preferable to treatment by persons untrained in chemical dependency; I suspect that the rate of spontaneous remission is greater for the untreated than it is for the mistreated. Certainly, those who are

---

2. The use of adolescent peer counselors who have no formal training in therapy, or, for that matter, are still in secondary school, has its apologists. I am not one of them. The idea that untrained adolescent counselors are superior to trained professionals is absurd.

mistreated are in greater jeopardy than those who are untreated. Those persons who are most likely to mistreat the chemical dependent are those who are or who have been affected by chemical dependency themselves, and who themselves have never been treated. I suppose this includes just about everybody.

I advocate serial and concurrent combinations of family, group, and individual treatment on the premise that the client, already confused by the absence of information, will only benefit from its acquisition. I trust in the competence of my clients to store and sort the information received.

Within the environment of the treatment chosen, the following hierarchy of focus, working from the present to the past, is strongly recommended. Each level includes work on the cycle of client's feelings, behavior that follows those feelings, and feeling and behavioral reactions to the client's behavior by the network of family and community that surrounds the client.

1. The Client's Own Use of Chemicals

Any use of mood-altering chemicals will confound and delay healing and growth. It has increasingly been my custom to ask family members of the person who is chemically dependent to refrain from the use of mood-altering drugs (including sugar and nicotine) while they and/or the client are in treatment. Occasionally, a teenage client who is in minor trouble with his or her own drinking can be seduced into sobriety and abstinence by focusing on a parent's drinking or drugging. This is usually referred to as the "back door" by those Al-Anon and Alateen members who enter these groups prior to joining Alcoholics Anonymous or Narcotics Anonymous.

2. Use of Chemicals by the Clients Family

When the client's own use of mood-altering drugs has been dealt with and the client has demonstrated continued ability to remain abstinent, the focus may profitably shift to issues involving the current use of chemicals by persons in the client's household or family of procreation. This usually involves the client's spouse if an adult or the parent if the client is a child. It is not necessary for all members of the household to become clean and sober before progressing to the next stage. But it is necessary to find ways of coping with the behaviors of the chemically dependent which are healthy for all concerned.

3. Use of Chemicals in the Historical Family

Only when issues surrounding the current use of chemicals by the client and her household have been examined and dealt with is it appropriate to deal with distant issues involving family of origin. These include adult children of alcoholics issues as well as all those psychodynamic issues so dear to traditionally trained psychotherapists. Therapists who are seduced by these issues and insist on their premature treatment will not, in the long run, be effective for their clients.

The therapist who insists on treating child sexual abuse issues, for example, before treating chemical addiction and compulsive eating/bingeing, puts his client in life jeopardy. The issues surrounding child sexual abuse are complex and fascinating. The clients are often needy of all the therapist's talents. Therapy, however, involves dealing with pain. Nothing is more painful than having been sexually used or abused. The addicted client tries to avoid the pain of therapy through self-medication. She or he returns to those addictive behaviors known best, becoming physically more and more ill with every visit to the therapist.

Paradoxically, a problem at this level will often be the problem that brings the client to treatment. On the other hand, counselors who are well trained in the treatment of chemical dependency but not trained in traditional therapies may deny that any work at this level is necessary in order to maintain sobriety. I believe that significant awareness of the family of origin is crucial to long term, contented sobriety, especially if the client has a parent or grandparent with a history of chemical dependency.

4. Chemical Use in the Historical Families of Persons Other Than the Client

The final level of attention concerns the chemical behavior in the families of origin of those close to the client. This usually concerns intimate, interpersonal behavior of one's spouse or partner that has its roots in the chemical dependency or other dysfunction of the partner's parents. This is the level where co-dependency issues of intimacy and control are most often treated.

Since it is rare for most adult children of alcoholics to escape either becoming alcoholic or marrying one, implicit in this heirarchy of treatment is the idea that for most adult children of alcoholics, active participation in Alcoholics Anonymous or traditional, spouse oriented Al-Anon is *initially* more appropriate and necessary than is participation in groups of Adult Children of Alcoholics or Codependents Anonymous. The adult child whose consumption of alcohol or other drugs is problematic or abusive *and* who chooses an ACOA/Al-Anon/CODA group over Alcoholics Anonymous is playing a dangerous game of hide-and-seek.

Another implicit assumption is that each person giving treatment has completed significant personal work at each of the above levels. Without such work, the professional jeopardizes his or her own recovery as well as that of the client.

Termination of formal treatment is suggested when the client has spontaneously demonstrated an ability to cope with the crises of everyday life without chemicals. Each such ability should be self-sustaining, with each coping skill leading to the development of new skills. The only requirement is that each coping skill be, in psychological terms, adaptive and functional. This usually begins to happen when the client comes into a series of sessions, and with considerable glee presents his/her problems, the possible solutions, the process by which the ultimate solution was achieved, and the adaptive solution already in place, without prior consultation with the therapist. What these clients have done, in fact, has been to replace the negative system (dysfunctional spiral) with a positive, growth spiral.

Since this process is a self-sustaining chain reaction, formal treatment is often quite short (six to eighteen months) and inexpensive. Further treatment with other therapists or educators may be sampled at leisure in order to accelerate and enhance the growth process.

9

...

The Care and Management of Flashbacks

There is hardly an adult who has never experienced a flashback. Flashbacks come without warning, taking your breath away like you've been hit in the stomach. You go downstairs into a musty cellar, and all the musty cellars of your youth return in an instant. Your child does something wrong, and you yell at the kid and all of a sudden it comes back to you that you said exactly what your parent said—and you had sworn on all that's holy that you would never, ever say anything like that to your kids when you grew up. You're driving alone down the road, and you pass a house like the one you lived in as a child, and you burst into tears for no reason at all.

Briefly defined, a flashback is the return to one's memory of a past event that has been repressed from memory for some time. The flashback is instantaneous, triggered by a current stimulus, and may involve one, all or none of the senses: sight, hearing, smell, and taste. It comes without warning. The impact of its arrival leaves you breathless. The pain of it is enough to make you cry when you haven't shed a tear in years. Flashbacks intrude on your day-to-day life, demanding immediate attention. They take energy away from the performance of daily tasks, and last from a few seconds to several hours. In some cases, parts of the former event are relived, and you may repeat behaviors previously repressed.

You may be terrorized by some of these flashbacks. They make you relive pain you would rather keep buried. In addition to the pain of the flashback, you may experience feelings of helplessness and loss of control, because the flashback comes without warning.

The repressed material often comes from a childhood of neglect or abuse. Repression is a useful psychological defense mechanism because it banishes from awareness those feelings which are too painful or anxiety producing for the child to handle. A twenty-seven-year-old woman, who was from age six physically and emotionally abused by alcoholic parents, writes, "I have frequent flashbacks. They are filled with the pain I knew. They are caused by the recurrence of the attitudes and occasionally by catchwords and gestures which remind me in unprotected moments of incidents in the past."

A childhood of chronic and multiple traumas you were powerless to handle contains many repressed events and feelings. As a child in an alcoholic or abusive family, you probably did not have the emotional skill to process painful events. So you repressed them and survived another day.

However, you paid a price for repression. This price was paid in psychological energy. Psychological energy spent on repression is no longer available for other purposes. The energy involved in the repressed feelings is also tied up and unavailable to you. Your ability to perform, be creative, or indulge in certain behaviors may be severely limited. The amnesia of large periods of childhood so many children of alcoholics experience is an example of repression.

My own experience may help you lessen the terror of flashbacks when they appear, and, instead, use them as a tool for recovery.

One of the first things I noticed about flashbacks was that they involved good memories as well: good times, good sex, good play, good company. Like the painful flashbacks, the good flashbacks occurred at the wrong time. I would have pleasant flashbacks when I was with a client, when I had important work to do, in the middle of a conversation, and so forth. So I said to myself, "this is really a pleasant memory. I don't have time to enjoy it now, but I will bring it up later this afternoon when I will be able to really get into it." And that's what I did.

This process is called suppression. Like repression, it postpones dealing with an unpleasant event; but unlike repression, it does not avoid dealing with the event entirely.

At other times, I had the opportunity at the onset of the flashback to enjoy the feelings I was experiencing. It was especially nice when I could share these experiences with someone close to me as they were happening.

It then occurred to me that one of the reasons that painful flashbacks were so terrifying to me was that they kept coming back, despite my efforts to keep them repressed. What would happen if I let these memories reappear and hang around for a while?

What happened was that as I relived the event, I was very sad. Sometimes I got angry about the event, but mostly I felt sad, lonely, and very vulnerable. Much later I was able to cry, but in the early days, my eyes would fill with tears that were never let go.

The feelings never lasted long, although they were intense while they were there. By allowing myself to experience these feelings, I understood what it was like for me as a child and how powerless I had really been. I found that what I seem to have needed most as a child was to be listened to and given a big hug. As an adult, I could listen to my pain and be my own parent. I could then either ask for a hug from someone close to me, or give the child within me a mental hug.

At this point I began to understand that the flashbacks were not an enemy to be repressed. Instead, I realized that flashbacks meant that my mind was now capable of handling whatever had been repressed. I was no longer a child; I had resources that had not been available to me when I was little.

I discovered that I may operate safely under the assumption that my mind is essentially healthy, that my mind wants to get better. The mind's priority to heal itself comes before all other events, no matter how important those events may be.

Fundamental to the care and management of flashbacks is the understanding that the events themselves are less important than the feelings that surround them. Feelings must be processed, and before they can be processed they must be felt. We are *not* out of control when we feel. Paradoxically, it is only when we allow ourselves to face the full range of our emotional experience that we are truly in control.

Many adult children of alcoholics experience partial or total amnesia of their childhood. This is not a happening to be ashamed of—it is only evidence of a need to survive. Yet, there are consequences. Consider that one's identity is formed from the sum of one's life experiences. To lose memory of those experiences is to lose contact with significant portions of one's identity. We are less afraid to tell people who we are than we are *unable* to tell people who we are. We will not know who we are until we uncover our past. Flashbacks are nature's way of restoring our identity.

After fifteen years in recovery, the flashbacks still come. I still have a mass of repressed material to deal with. The easiest way for me to induce a flashback is to identify with someone at a meeting. The most powerful self-induced flashbacks are those stimulated by the poetry of alcoholism. These are the flashbacks over which I have the most control, because I control their initiation. Other stimuli are aroused by guided imagery and by going to self-help group meetings.

When major flashbacks arrive at the wrong time, I say, "Not now, I'll deal with this later." I set a time and place to deal with the returning material. Then I share with friends or my therapist or my group what I have experienced. I receive love and support that as a child I never knew existed. One person I know says that when he has a flashback, he incorporates into it acknowledgment and support, so that if the flashback reappears, it comes back with that support and acknowledgment.

I deal with minor flashbacks as they come up, often in seconds. Dealing with flashbacks is a skill one develops over time. As a result, my childhood amnesia has, by and large, disappeared. I know what has happened to me and who I am. I have more energy than I ever thought possible, and I am very thrifty with the amount of psychological energy I am willing to spend on unnecessary things.

10 ...

Feelings

When I stopped drinking, I discovered that I had had no feelings. What I did have was a lot of behaviors that were reactions to phenomena that I later found out were feelings. When I was angry, I drank. When I celebrated, I drank. When I was anxious, I drank to dissolve the knots in my stomach. (It didn't work.) When I was happy, I drank. When I was tired, I drank to reward myself. When I was sick, I drank to nurture myself. In short, whenever I experienced a feeling of any kind, I attempted to neutralize the feeling with alcohol.

This had several practical side effects. The first was that whenever I medicated my feelings, I could not learn from them. We are given feelings so that we may alter our behavior in healthy directions. Thus, pain is given us so that we may learn to avoid injury. Our funnybone is given to us to release us from our sorrows, and so on. I, on the other hand, was a classic case of arrested emotional development. None of the anger I had accumulated in my childhood could be appropriately expressed. My deadened and anesthetized feelings could not teach me or guide my daily life.

Feelings have several important properties that, when known, help us to regain access to them. Feelings are neither good, bad, shameful, or awful. It's not shameful to have a feeling. Most children of alcoholics have wished at one time or another that their parents were dead, and that they had killed them. The act of killing is wrong. The feeling isn't. Just because we have a feeling, we don't have to act on it. I may have sexual or erotic feelings toward half the women I encounter. It's inappropriate to act out these feelings. I can, however, enjoy them. And I do.

Feelings are ephemeral. They just don't last long. Feelings have a tendency to evaporate in time, unless we hold on to them and nourish them. If we choose to nourish anger and hate, they will stick around. If we choose to nourish love and compassion, love and compassion will be our companions. But mostly, feelings don't stick around long. They're transient and expendable.

Feelings are energy. As energy, they can be stored for use later, or the energy they represent can be used in the present. The energy stored by repressed feelings is not available to us for current use. Once the feelings have been expressed, the energy becomes available. That is why catharsis, or the ventilation of previously repressed feelings, can involve the expenditure of tremendous amounts of energy. It's the knowledge, even the subconscious knowledge that repressed feelings involve so much energy that we are afraid of letting our feelings out. We are afraid that we or someone else will be destroyed in the process. It is for this reason that Bataca bats and pillows were invented—to provide a safe outlet for feelings long repressed.

Feelings can be changed. They can be replaced with other feelings. If you have access to your feelings, and know how they work, you can change them at will.

Feelings are useful and necessary to life itself. If it were not for feelings, we would not be able to change our behavior or modify our habits to meet changing circumstances. Were it not for the pain of hunger, we would never eat. Were it not for the pleasures of sex, we would not reproduce.

Feelings are not the person. If I have a bad feeling, I am not bad. If I feel ashamed, I am not shameful. If I have a good feeling, I am not *necessarily* a good person, although I may be.

Children of alcoholics tend to run from feelings. They tend to squash feelings, especially new ones. These are instantly perceived as "bad," rather than different. For example, rather than experience a feeling of acceptance, we will reject the person who offers it. Rather than enter a new relationship that might be temporary, we stay away from that person because we can't stand the idea of experiencing feelings of loss, and in doing so we deprive ourselves of some very enriching relationships. Feelings of love, sex, intimacy, and touching tend to be confused in the adolescent and adult child's mind. Feelings of sadness, despair, loneliness, depression, loss, and grief also tend to be merged into one blue lump. Our feelings, both high and low, are so often perceived as uncomfortable that we medicate them with alcohol and other drugs.

What to do with feelings? The purpose of feelings is to feel them. There's no way out. In order to be alive, we need to allow ourselves to feel the feeling, to experience it in all its dimensions, trusting that we will not be destroyed by it. No feeling is too much to handle, though we may need support from our friends when the pain is great. Feelings are there to be shared. Our friends cannot make the facts that contributed to our feelings change, but they can be there for us if we will let them. They can help us to work our feelings through. We need to let our feelings go. Feelings are there to be explored in all their dimensions. The natural history of a feeling has a beginning and an end. Those of us who are adept at squashing feelings always squash them in the beginning of the feeling. We never allow ourselves to feel the end. Feelings are there to be experienced all the way through. The only way to do that, sometimes, is to dig in your heels and not run for cover. Do not hold on to them and repress them, but just let them go.

OK, so how do you let go? One way is to decide to trust the God of your understanding, your higher power. Imagine you are hanging by your fingertips from a cliff thousands of feet above the ground. If in your mind's eye, you can let go of the cliff edge, and trust your higher power to protect you, that is letting go. Of course, if you don't have a higher power, you are in serious trouble. Ellen Ratner says, "The concept of the spiritual, or God, is simply the idea that something or someone is with me and for me."[1] If you do not believe that your higher power is with you and for you, you are not going to let go. There is a paradox, here, as well as a double bind. If you do not risk, if you do not trust, if you do not let go, you will never find out whether or not there is something or someone who is with you and for you. On the other hand, if you

---

1. Ratner, Ellen. (1990). *The other side of the family.* Pompano Beach, FL: Health Communications.

are willing to do the hard work required to break out of the double bind, the results can be very powerful, indeed. This is the stuff of which spiritual awakenings are made.

If you've ever had an orgasm, you know how to let go. You let the tension build, and then you let it go. The feeling in the orgasm is very pleasant, but just physical. The feeling of letting go emotionally is infinitely more subtle and complex, and far more interesting than physical release.

Normally, feelings do not come with written guarantees. But if you understand the properties of feelings, you can be assured that you won't be destroyed; that although you may be uncomfortable, the feeling will end, and eventually you will feel better and have more energy.

Well, that's all very nice, but how does it explain why I'm so full of rage?

Rage is white lightning going from a stimulus to explosion in a microsecond. The response is always far greater than would normally be required by such an ordinary stimulus. Rage is reactive rather than purposeful, impulsive rather than planned. Rage destroys relationships, to say nothing of the self. How do we get that way?

This is the way I worked it out. Take a stimulus, any stimulus will do. Suppose you and I are visiting, and all of a sudden I get up and kick you in the shin. What's your very first feeling? No, it's not anger. Your first feelings are *hurt, surprise, disappointment,* and *betrayal.* You demand an explanation. "Why did you do that?" you ask. You want to feel better *now.* You want resolution, *now.* I, on the other hand, am not sensitive to your feelings. I don't respond to you. You ask me again. I still don't respond. Now, you are *frustrated.* You tell me that. You say, "Hey! You kicked me in the shin! That hurt! And you won't even tell me why! I thought we were friends! I feel frustrated." And still being insensitive and unfeeling, I respond, "So what?" and kick you in the shin again. Your chance for a resolution of this matter has been frustrated again. Now, you are *angry.* And you tell me that. "Hey, turkey, that's twice you've kicked me, and twice you've hurt me for no reason at all. That makes me very angry. I want you to apologize and promise you won't do it again." I continue to be insensitive, and as a reward for your assertiveness and patience, I give you another swift kick right where I've done it twice before. How do you feel now? Do this to a child a thousand times, and he, like me, will go from any unpleasant event evoking feelings of loss, hurt, or disappointment, to frustration to anger to rage, all in an instant. The process happens with such speed that it seems that all the intermediary steps are bypassed or tripped through with extraordinary rapidity.

How to deal with this? If you're the person experiencing the rage, you know there is a problem when you have to justify the results of your rage afterward. The amount of energy you expend and the consequences of your rage always exceed what would have been appropriate for the original stimulus. So the first clue that you're in trouble is when you justify your actions, and the second clue is when you realize that your reaction was inappropriate to the original problem. When I first discovered this mechanism, I prayed for time. I needed time between the original stimulus and my response so that I could figure out what was going on and apply the lessons I was learning in recovery. That's nothing more complicated than counting to ten before reacting.

But once I figured out the process outlined above, my responses could become much more sophisticated.

But first, I had to work on the old stuff. The past hurts that remained unresolved needed to be attended to. Some were let go, like employees being laid off. The energy expense of keeping them around was too great. The energy of other unresolved hurts was expressed in therapy and in groups, beaten to death with Bataka bats and pillows, or transformed to useful endeavors. I went through four years of graduate school on old anger, and when the old anger was gone, I stopped going to school. Sometimes resolution was achieved through confronting the perpetrators in my life, either the real ones or symbolic substitutes. Some hurts were disposed of simply because I was validated, or amends were made to me. A new crop of hurts, of course, was harvested every year, and I had to learn how to deal with them before they got to the rage stage. That meant becoming assertive. About this time, I was asked to teach a course in assertiveness for men, and so I taught myself by teaching others. In becoming assertive, I learned a great deal about truth in feelings.

11 ...

Parenting

Psychologists and ministers of religion should probably not have children. Their expectations for their progeny are sometimes too unrealistic. Nevertheless, I can now reveal that I am the parent of a wonderful five-year-old boy. As such, my perception has shifted radically from that of an outsider to that of an insider.

Parenting is not easy. The hard part comes from its loneliness, the necessity of learning and doing something new every minute, every day. Our only experience in parenting is dimly remembered from what we learned from our own parents. What we can glean from whatever parenting books we have on hand we almost always glean when we're in crisis, with results that are less than perfect. When we're not in crisis, we're trying to get some sleep.

On the one hand, I really did think it would be easier. When Janice became pregnant, I promised her that the parenting would be fifty-fifty. I would have promised her anything for a child. My promise was sincere; my optimism was grounded in ignorance.

What I learned, and what Janice and other mothers confirm, is that every mother is a single parent. Nevertheless, I think that parenting is a two-person job. When one of us has difficulty coping, or is out of control, the other is usually in top form. The understanding that neither one of us ever wants to be truly a single parent provides significant motivation to work on our coupleship issues. It was Lee Silverstein who first told me that any two adults together are smarter than any kid. We've found that to be true. It may take us a while, but it's true.

Remember that I am the child of an alcoholic. When it comes to conflict, I'm as slippery as Teflon on ice. Conflict is the prospect of doing anything other than what I'm doing when I want to do what I'm doing. In other words, maintain the status quo and don't bother me.

That's the mind-set, and to overcome it takes a lot of energy. It helps when the kid is healthy. It helps when he's good-looking and cute. It helps when I'm healthy. It helps when I know myself and how my mind works.

It doesn't help matters when the kid is sick. It doesn't help when I'm sick. It doesn't help when I don't know what to do because nothing I've tried works. It doesn't help when I'm worried about where this month's rent is coming from. And it certainly won't help if I am drinking or stressed from someone else's drinking.

So what works? My approach to parenting is rather simplistic. Somehow, I got the idea that like other aspects of my recovery, parenting was a system. It could either be a positive system or a negative one. If I could set up the parameters of a positive system, my occasional failures as a parent would disappear into a sea of small successes and minor triumphs. Some of these things were done consciously, some with little or no forethought.

The best thing I ever did to prepare myself for parenting was to recover from my alcoholism and that of my parents. When Charlie was conceived, I had been sober for over ten years, and most of those years had been spent working on adult child issues. Recovery is the best school for parenting there is.

It wasn't so long ago that physicians would tell mothers that it was all right to drink one or two glasses of alcohol during pregnancy. Now only the most irresponsible doctor would make such a statement. We now know that even these small amounts have an adverse effect on the fetus. Our concern for the prenatal environment went so far as to exclude caffeine, diet soda, aspirin, and acetaminophen[1] from Janice's diet.

The first thing we did with Charlie was pick him up. I got mad at

---

1. A handy and informative guide to substances that can affect your unborn baby can be found in Kelley-Buchanan, C. *Peace of mind during pregnancy*. NY: Dell, 1988. Mothers should note that what physicians tell you is safe this year may have changed by the time your baby is born, when it is too late. It is better to do without a substance for nine months than to grieve taking it for a lifetime.

the nurse in the hospital because she wouldn't let us be with him enough. I wanted Charlie to be held, to be stroked, to be touched. I wanted him to know we were there. I wanted him to feel secure in our warmth. I wanted him to be free of anxiety and stress. Touching does all these things, and more.

Although my love for adults can often be conditional when I'm under stress, my love for Charlie has no strings attached. He simply could do no wrong as an infant. If he threw up all over my shirt, I cleaned it up and got another shirt. If I got poop on my fingers, I washed my hands. I didn't take it personally. Charlie did the things he did as a baby because he was a baby, and all babies do the things he did. It wasn't his fault. It wasn't my fault. It wasn't Janice's fault. It just was.

I think disposable diapers are wonderful. They kept Charlie dry and clean in a way that no other diaper can. By changing him the moment he was wet, Charlie was a year and a half old before he had his first diaper rash. I think that saved us a lot of grief, and Charlie a lot of pain and tears. I know that there are environmental considerations with disposables. I hope they can be worked out.

I learned from one of my therapists to lead by following. When Charlie was ready to be toilet trained, Charlie told us he was ready. It was a little later than I would have liked, but we had learned that if we followed his developmental schedule we would have fewer problems. Janice trained him solely through praise and positive reinforcement in this department. Accidents were (and continue to be) dismissed as simply accidents.

I want more than anything else for Charlie to have a relationship with his father. Janice and I are particularly fortunate in that we own our own business and work in it together. For the first five months of his life, Charlie was with us both for almost every waking moment. Even now, he is with us both from 5:30 in the evening until 9:00 in the morning. That's a lot of time with us that he wouldn't have if we were commuting to the city every day.

Time together is not enough to make a relationship. Please bear in mind that nothing bores me more than playing with children's toys, even with Charlie. My attention span is more limited than any child's when it comes to child's play. What I am able to do well is to maintain eye contact with Charlie when we talk about serious matters. Serious matters are his feelings, my feelings, his behavior, or my behavior. Eye contact is maintained by sitting him on my lap so that our heads are on the same plane. Anything can be a matter of discussion. This does not mean that he gets everything that he wants, but he does get taken seriously.

Given the impulsive nature of our syndrome, I am very concerned about personal safety. As a child I was accident prone. As a recovering person, I no longer permit myself to have accidents that are physically injurious. So it's "Safety First!" Once we had gotten the idea of personal safety across to Charlie (like everything else, through endless repetition) he would remind us constantly to put on our seat belts and to place both hands on the steering wheel of our car when driving.

I don't like being told what to do. I especially do not like being told what to do by a four or five-year old who is only repeating what I have taught him. Moral consistency takes precedence however, and I acknowledge my son's comments by doing as he requests. In doing so, I honor my son. He will not have to struggle with the conflict inherent in discriminating differences between what I say and what I do.

I know from my own recovery and from my clinical experience that modeling is the single most powerful teaching tool that I have.

Charlie so identifies with me that he wants to go on a diet like his dad, and at the same time he wants a big, soft belly, just like his dad. Isn't it nice that he doesn't have a model for smoking or getting drunk?

As a reaction to my childhood history and as a reaction to our war against Vietnam, I am no longer a militarist. I have abandoned the justification of violence as a method of resolving conflict. The result is that Charlie gets spanked only when *I* am out of control, only when my knowledge of what is really going on is deficient. Spanking conveys the message that I can use pain to control or to punish. I want my boy to grow into a caring, compassionate, gentle man. Spanking provides teaching that is inconsistent with this goal. Besides, it doesn't work.

Will we be successful as parents? A few months ago, I watched Charlie enter his day-care center and spontaneously give a classmate a hug. He learned this at four years of age. I learned how to hug in my late thirties. I think that Charlie has a head start in life.

I once received a letter suggesting that we were less than adequate parents for placing our child in a day-care center. I think that this notion is absurd. For the first five months of his life, Charlie lived in our bookstore.[2] The environment was boring, dangerous, and inappropriate. We placed him with a baby-sitter who gave him unconditional love in the company of other children. When this was no longer possible, we found a day-care center that provided an enriching and challenging environment while remembering that childhood is a time for play.

The day-care center reflects our values and is not a warehouse for unhappy children. As a result, Charlie has thrived in this setting. The local school, we have heard, is now complaining that the day-care students are more advanced than those who did not have the opportunities we have had. But what is more important than our reflected glory in our children's accomplishments is the fact that Charlie comes into contact with two parents who, at the beginning and end of their day, are on their best behavior.

I think that parenting is extremely demanding. It is hard work, both physically and emotionally. To demand that a parent from a dysfunctional family system spend one-hundred percent of his and her waking hours with a child is to contribute inevitably to the perpetuation of family dysfunction from one generation to another.

The child in a parenting/day-care system has the ability to acquire the experience of alternative models of behavior. When I was a child growing up in the Adirondacks, I had three sets of surrogate parents. One set was alcoholic. All provided unconditional love. At least one set of surrogate parents, I was to find out much later, had a pretty good idea of what my home life was like. They very consciously chose to provide an alternative, and treated me with as much love and discipline as they did their own son. I attribute much of the positive outcome of my life to their collective influence. It is my hope that Charlie will integrate the positive aspects of both his birth parents while rejecting the negative aspects of each.

We knew when Charlie was conceived that, given generations of alcoholism and drug dependence behind him, that his chances of being an alcoholic were very high, if not absolute. If this is his destiny, what are we to do as parents?

---

2. Whatever its deficiencies, growing up in a bookstore is infinitely better than spending one's adolescence in assorted barrooms, which was my experience.

From the very earliest, the quality of our relationship became a high priority. If Charlie gets into trouble with alcohol, the quality of our relationship needs to be such that we are credible in his eyes. Will this relationship withstand the rigors of male adolescence? I don't know. But if our record as parents is one of long-term consistency in love, honesty, and respect, I think we increase the odds that we will be listened to in a time of crisis.

When I began drinking, there was no clear line of demarcation between the pain caused by my drinking and the pain in my family. If Charlie chooses to drink alcohol, and that drinking causes him pain, I want to be sure that his pain is significantly different from the feelings he encountered as a child in our family. That way, it may be clear to him that there are significant consequences resulting from his drinking.

This also means that if Charlie gets into trouble through his behavior, we do not further his dysfunction through our enabling behaviors. Enabling behaviors are anything that allow a person to avoid the natural consequences of his actions. That means we don't lie, cover up, protect, or allow ourselves to be manipulated in furtherance of dysfunctional behavior.

Our position as parents is somewhat different than my mother's. My mother's dramatic recovery from alcoholism provided a powerful model for change. Charlie has a good chance to grow up never having seen his parents smoke cigarettes, drink alcohol, get drunk, or need to recover from any of these. His model for recovery will, I hope, have been integrated from birth—high self-esteem, immediate access to his feelings, and healthy coping skills. We shall see. In the meantime, my only regret is that we are somewhat old to consider having another child. I console myself by remembering that more of a good thing is not necessarily a good thing.

In any discussion on parenting, it is probably wiser and more prudent not to blow one's horn too loudly. That's why our expertise in parenting is limited to the experience of the last four to five years. Like any parents, we are proud of the abilities and accomplishments of our child. But it is important to note that these are his abilities and accomplishments and not ours. We are not enhanced or diminished by his performance. Charlie is going to have enough trouble discovering and living up to his own expectations without being obligated to live up to ours. I'm proudest when Charlie can tell us that he is scared or sad, when he spontaneously hugs us, when he shares his love for another, and when he plays a joke on his old man. The worth of these simple things cannot be calculated. But if we can continue to teach these simple things, then we as parents will be content.

12 ...

How to Change the World for Twenty-Five Dollars or Less

About five years ago, a group of my students at Mater Dei College in Ogdensburg, New York embarked on a rather unusual exercise. The task put to my students, after three days of instruction on the dynamics of alcoholism in the family, was to perform an alcoholism intervention at the community level. After dividing into five groups of five persons each, the students were told that they had one hour to agree upon the intervention of their choice.

The only parameters for the intervention were that no group could spend more than twenty-five dollars, or five dollars per person, and that the intervention had to be started and completed between 1 P.M. and 5 P.M. that day.

The immediate effects of this exercise were interesting. The students could not indulge in grandiose plans, expensive in time, money and resources (and therefore guaranteed to fail or remain unfinished forever). No grants could be sought, no promises could be made, and the future was not a factor. The time and money limitations forced the students to focus on the practical and the possible.

What they accomplished in the few hours on that hot summer afternoon has had long-lasting effects. One group started an adult children of alcoholics meeting, which continues today. That group fostered many splinter groups in both Canada and the United States. Another group arranged for a newspaper article on adult children of alcoholics, which was printed the following morning.

The same group also persuaded the local radio stations to run public service announcements for the self-help group. One group wrote letters on Fetal Alcohol Syndrome to all the local hospitals, offering themselves as a resource. Some wrote letters to their local newspapers, letters that were published and resulted in many referrals.

Other interventions included the donation of several copies of Cathleen Brooks's *The Secret Everyone Knows*[1] to the Boys Club and the creation of posters illustrating the needs of children of alcoholics to be placed on school bulletin boards. Total cost of the afternoon's activities was under sixteen dollars.

Perhaps the most extraordinary intervention, however, was that performed by the students on themselves. Each group had resolved, for a moment, the conflict between compulsion and practicality and had acquired considerable self-esteem in the process. They reported that their feelings of helplessness disappeared and were replaced by confidence in their ability to create change.

There is something to this "One Day at a Time" business. Perhaps if we look to what we can accomplish today we will avoid the creation of bureaucracies which feed egos but fail to address the pain in our souls.

---

1. Brooks, C. (1981). *The secret everyone knows*. Center City, MN: Hazelden.

13 ...

Forgiving Our Parents

Can alcoholic parents ever be forgiven by their children for what happened during the course of active alcoholism?

Children of alcoholics have a vested interest in forgiveness. When we become stubborn with our forgiveness, we become stuck and stagnant. Being stuck is painful. Blaming extends the pain.

When I moved away from home, I was silent and unforgiving for four years. No visits, no telephone calls, no cards, no letters, no holidays, no birthdays. Just alienation and emptiness. When others spoke of visiting their parents for the holidays, I wondered why anyone would want to do that. One day, I showed up on my alcoholic's doorstep, without explanation, just as if nothing had ever happened. That's what untreated COAs do when they deny their pain.

The Twelve Step groups taught me that detachment does not mean abandonment. Separation bought me only loneliness and emptiness, to be medicated with booze.

When I separated my pain from my other feelings, I naturally and appropriately got angry over my childhood treatment. By paying attention to the pain I was reliving, I could deal with it in new ways. Sharing the pain with others was one. It was really that bad. My childhood experiences were not appropriate or healthy. I was affected. My daily habits were rooted in my past. I could not turn back the clock; the scars I bore were real. In my grief, I cursed my parents and the fate that brought us together in the same family.

Then I realized that my parents, whatever their faults, were no different, no worse and no better than I. I couldn't apply different standards to them. But they were my parents! They should have known better! The facts are they didn't know better. As a sober alcoholic, I knew that my own life management problems were most often rooted in ignorance and lack of skill, instead of weakness or psychological defect. How could I apply different standards to my parents? My ego must be fragile and overblown, indeed, if I persist in demanding better, more knowledgeable, more perfect parents than anyone else. Not wanting a fragile and overblown ego, I gave up the notion that my parents must be perfect. Conversations with sober friends taught me that active alcoholics always did the very best they knew how or were capable of at the time. They were responsible only for their recovery, not for becoming alcoholic. I had a choice. I could reject my parents' humanity only at the price of rejecting my own.

I date the beginning of my recovery from the time that one of my parents told me of their alcoholism. The fact of their being able to change made a very profound and lasting impression. I had thought I was a *fait accompli*. My character, I thought, was set in stone, immutable until death. Their recovery upset that notion. Of all the healing things that have happened to me, one of the strongest and most influential was knowing that change is possible.

An essential ingredient of my relationships with other people, especially children, is the ability to admit that I am wrong—not after I am confronted with the facts of my error by someone else, but before.

My fears about any damage I may do to my children or other young people around me are lessened by the knowledge that it does not have to continue, that I am capable of change. What I don't know I can learn. The best source of learning about parenting is from other parents (found at the PTA, Twelve-Step Meetings, day care, adult education classes, etc.). Books are often helpful in providing insight at leisure and for organizing material. However, the most efficient method of dispelling fear, denial, and ignorance is to educate oneself in the company of others.

Some children of alcoholics never work through the pain. They expend all their energy in blaming. They fantasize that their parents will notice their anger, and once having noticed it, will stop drinking, admit that they were wrong, and everybody will live happily ever after. These children of alcoholics waste the better part of their lives in bitterness and recrimination.

With time, their investment of energy in the blaming process becomes so great that it reinforces the state of being stuck. To change from a mode of controlling and blame to the forgiveness of letting go requires too much energy, too much loss of pride. Whatever self-esteem is left is wrapped up in being better than the alcoholic. Self-growth is abandoned in favor of waiting for others to change. That can be a long wait!

Look at it this way. Suppose I was crossing the street one day, and a driver went through a red light and knocked me down, and my leg was broken. Not only did I have physical damage, but I experienced a fair amount of psychological trauma. Everybody who witnessed the accident testifies that I was blameless, and that the driver was at fault. The driver will be judged judicially, and with a little luck, will get his due from the court. I, on the other hand, still have a broken leg and some psychological scar tissue. No amount of judicial action will repair my leg or my psyche. I am the one who must take responsibility for my physical and emotional therapy, whether or not the system requires the driver to pay for it. I am the only one who can make me better. And getting better is such an important issue for me that I will not allow anyone, especially a perpetrator, to get in the way of my recovery. If that means letting go of my anger and blame so that I can proceed along my therapeutic course, then so be it.

Does that mean I must forget? Not in a thousand years! If anything, I'm even less likely to forget. Because I have been injured, I now set boundaries so that I will not be injured again. Some of my boundaries are territorial: enter only at my invitation, otherwise stay away. You may not destroy or damage my person or my property. Some of my boundaries are emotional: do not manipulate me, use me, or abuse me. Treat me ethically and responsibly. If you cannot do these things, then our present and future relationship must necessarily be limited. I take responsibility for setting the limits and boundaries. It is up to others to respect those limits and boundaries. If someone chooses to violate them, they do so at their own risk and peril.

But what about forgiving those persons whose behaviors toward us were truly evil? The evil person is the one who uses knowledge of good to do bad. There are such persons. My guess is that while few of them are alcoholic, some may be. The hard part is that I have no right to judge what goes on in another's mind and soul, if only because my own access to that mind and soul is limited. Judgment at such a level must inevitably wait for that dimension of space and time that follows death. In the meantime, I have my own recovery to worry about. If I can let go of my need to hate, to blame, and to judge, then I believe I have confounded evil, which is indeed a delicious and wonderful paradox.

Epilogue

Mom lives in Florida, having worked stints as alcoholism counselor, beachcomber, alcoholism counselor, frame-shop operator, professional photographer, and alcoholism counselor, in that order. She's sober for twenty continuous years in Alcoholics Anonymous. Both of her best friends back home died from alcoholism. Despite her involvement with AA, Mom's still an atheist. Personally, I think she would be better off not being an atheist. However, I delight in using her as an example to those who use their atheism or agnosticism as an excuse for not getting sober in AA. In any event, her beliefs or lack of them are none of my business. Mom has birthed me twice, the last time facilitating my recovery from alcoholism. She's been to ACOA meetings and has begun to deal with her family of origin. I think she's a little nervous about my writing this book, but she has nothing to be ashamed of.

At Easter of 1990, my father was dry a year. He told me he'd had an accident while driving drunk, having run into a tree. A month later he decided he'd "had his fling" and stopped drinking. He also stopped smoking. All this at the age of seventy-five. I'm sure my father was not responsible for becoming an alcoholic. I'm equally sure that his community had a great deal to do with enabling his active alcoholism for so many decades. From time to time, he would be stopped by the New York State Police for driving while intoxicated. Instead of arresting him, they sent him back to the bar, and warned the tavern against serving him. A few days before Easter, Dad was discharged from the hospital after having been operated on for a cancer on his jaw. He knows the cancer was caused by his drinking and smoking. He's proud of his remarkable constitution, and doesn't think he needed or needs any help or therapy for his drinking. He's given up his home in the woods and moved into a retirement community. The other residents there never knew him as a drunk, and treat him like royalty. His charm is boyish, Irish, and impossible to resist. I once believed that if Dad ever got sober, I would really let him have it. I would confront him with everything that ever happened to me and my brother and sister. Well, I haven't and I won't. Dad seems to have found some internal peace, and I won't disturb it. I won't say that all the pain has disappeared. I chose to go back home to finish this book, and I've been having flashbacks so often that I have to get up every now and then and go tackle that woodpile. But I got my power back a long time ago. I'm resolved. What I really want to do is write mystery stories. That's probably what I'll try next.

APPENDIX 1

Suggestions for Adult Children's Groups

During the summer of 1981, I sat down on a Long Island beach and checked off the meetings in the *World Directory of Al-Anon Family Groups and Alateens* that were for Adult Children of Alcoholics. There were just eleven groups in seven states for adults then. Al-Anon groups for young people too old for Alateen numbered twenty-four in twelve states and two Canadian provinces.

Today, there are over a thousand Adult Children groups listed with Al-Anon in New York. Others are affiliated with Adult Children of Alcoholics (ACA) on the West Coast and many groups are independent, choosing not to be allied under any umbrella. Whatever their affiliation, Adult Children are coming together to heal the wounds of past traumas and to discover new ways of coping with life's difficulties.

I believe that self-help groups patterned on the model of Alcoholics Anonymous have all the healing qualities described by students of group dynamics.[1] By definition, self-help groups are led by laypersons rather than professionals. The lay therapy of Alcoholics Anonymous and the groups patterned after it has evolved into a slow—but safe—therapeutic medium.

The self-help groups I have come to know over the last ten years

---

1. I strongly suggest that professionals and laypersons alike should read the fourth chapter (The Therapeutic Factors: An Integration) in Yalom, I. (1985). *The theory and practice of group psychotherapy.* (3rd Edition) New York: Basic Books, before dismissing out of hand the therapeutic qualities of self-help groups. I also strongly suggest that any helping professional who conducts therapy groups and who has *not* read Yalom's work runs the risk, sooner or later, of malpractice.

generally follow a set format or skeleton structure that allows for a wide variety of therapeutic group experiences. The structure of the meeting provides a predictable and comforting ritual, allowing each participant an opportunity to hear and be heard. Sustained, steady attendance at meetings allows learning to be integrated. Integrated learning, in turn, leads to permanent, rather than superficial changes in behavior. What was once unmanageable becomes manageable and the changes are often dramatic.

Groups for Adult Children of Alcoholics are so new that many groups are formed by persons who have no prior self-help group experience. These groups, unsure of themselves and lacking the arrogance of the recovering alcoholic who needs only a resentment and a coffeepot to start a new AA meeting, sometimes flounder, thinking that they are doing something wrong. In reality, they are only reinventing a program of recovery founded a little over fifty years ago. Adult children of alcoholics groups, in terms of their evolutionary development, are today in the same place that AA was when AA was just a few years old.[2]

Other groups are composed of old-time members of AA and of Al-Anon, with a sprinkling of newcomers. These members often are shocked and confused by the intensity of experience and feeling that one encounters at an ACOA meeting. Like many children of alcoholics, they initially perceive as unpleasant those events (such as feelings of closeness and intimacy) that were theretofore foreign to them. Their shock turns to wonder when they realize that the self-help groups that have previously done so much for them (such as saving their lives and sanity) have not and cannot do what ACOA will do for them. The saying that ACOA is graduate school compared to Al-Anon and AA has much to commmend it. Some old-time AA members, believing that ACOA's have nothing to give up, may refuse to recognize the existence of adult children's groups or cooperate with them. Many Al-Anon members will exercise their control issues and attempt to legislate adult children's groups out of existence.

I hope that ACOA's growing pains will be relatively short. ACOA groups are learning from their experiences at a far faster rate than their parent AA and Al-Anon groups. It is a wise parent who can accept that the child often surpasses the achievements of the parents. It is a humble child who pays tribute to the parent for a path well prepared.

ACOA groups will sooner or later face the question of affiliation. Their

---

2. The reader who is familiar with the growing pains of ACOA groups (see Appendix 2) may profit from reading the similar experiences of AA, as recounted in [Wilson, W.G.] (1957). *Alcoholics anonymous comes of age*. New York: Alcoholics Anonymous World Services, Inc., in particular the section on Tradition Nine, pp. 118–123.

choice is to become part of Al-Anon Family Groups, Inc., headquartered in New York City, of Adult Children of Alcoholics, Inc., located in the Los Angeles area, or to remain independent. The advantage of affiliation with either Al-Anon or ACA is the added networking that enables prospective members to find the group. ACOA members who are active members of Alcoholics Anonymous may not be delegates to the Al-Anon World Service Conference or serve in any office above the group level. On the other hand, active alcoholics who are not members of AA may serve in such capacities. Al-Anon prefers that outside literature not be distributed at its meetings; however, each group is free to decide its own policy. Al-Anon will not sanction any literature not written under the direction of its headquarters and approved by its World Service Conference. Adult Children of Alcoholics, Inc. has no vested interest in any publication and has a policy of leaving the choice of literature up to each individual group.

One way of neatly sidestepping threats to group autonomy by a local service arm (Al-Anon Intergroup) is to form an Adult Children of Alcoholics Intergroup on a local or regional level under the Al-Anon umbrella. Such an Intergroup can function in the same territory as other Intergroups, without being distracted by the control issues that currently plague the present situation. This solution combines all the advantages of staying within the Al-Anon framework with none of the disadvantages.

Group Officers

Successful self-help groups have a number of persons among whom the responsibilities for conducting the group's business are shared. Elections (or group appointments) are best held every three to six months. Groups that hold on to their leaders for more extended periods of time tend to fall sick and die. Six months is just long enough for most controlling personalities to realize that what was originally fantasized as inspired leadership is in reality a commitment to sustained responsibility. Committing one's energies to an ACOA group tends to breed character and humility, but only if the term of office is limited. Persons chosen as officers should have at least six months of recovery. If the group is too new to have many persons with experience this long, the group might consider electing officers every three months.

CHAIRPERSON

Opens and closes the meeting. Carries the key to the meeting place. Outsiders think he/she is a big wheel. It ain't so.

PROGRAM CHAIRPERSON

Finds persons to lead small groups and/or to pick discussion topics. If program chairperson procrastinates or if the group leader doesn't show up, he/she fills the obligation him/herself. Sometimes this function is combined with that of chairperson.

GREETERS

It helps to designate one or two persons as the group's official greeters. The greeters stand by the door and welcome new and regular members of the group. It's also helpful if the greeters introduce newcomers to older members of the group. Greeters significantly reduce feelings of isolation and alienation among new members.

TREASURER

Responsible for the group's funds. Takes the basket after it is passed, counts and records funds received. Maintains group's bank account, if any. Orders and pays for literature. Personal borrowing from the group's funds, even when intending to pay it back, is called embezzlement. Don't do it! Successful groups never have more than one-hundred dollars in the kitty after rent and literature expenses have been met. The group conscience decides the disposition of excess funds.

SECRETARY

Keeper of the key or combination to the group's post office box. Reads any announcements at the meeting. Responsible for keeping literature and group records.

BOOKER

Some meetings may trade speakers from another meeting. It is the booker's responsibility to find speakers from his/her group willing to take the responsibility of speaking at another meeting. If the booker cannot find anyone to do this, the booker personally fills the committment.

STEERING COMMITTEE

Composed of current and past officers of the group. Acts as executive committee. Nominates new officers to be elected by the group at a business meeting. Business meetings are usually held following the group's regular meeting, and are announced as such. The purpose of the business meeting is to decide group policy as determined by the group conscience. Any person who says he/she is a member of the group is qualified to vote at a business meeting. The group conscience is the ultimate authority in the group.

Other Considerations

AUTHORITIES

It is inappropriate and unethical for any outside person, group, inter-group, organization, world service office, or helping professional to dictate how an individual self-help group conducts its affairs. Each group is independent and autonomous. Its survival depends on it!

MEETING PLACE

I sometimes think that the only proper function of churches is to provide basements where self-help groups can meet. The rent is usually cheap, the meeting place is well known and easily accessible. Storage space for the group's literature and coffeepot can usually be negotiated. Fixtures like tables and chairs are provided with rent. Other meeting places that have been successfully employed are union meeting halls, hospital cafeterias, bookstores, and schools. The choice of a church of any denomination for a meeting place does not mean that the church is affiliated or influences the group any more than the listing of your name in a telephone book suggests that you are affiliated with the telephone company.

PROPERTY

Groups tend to get into trouble if they own property other than literature and a coffeepot. Each group should be self-supporting through its collection basket, but should not have any great need for funds. If it has a surplus of funds, it might consider a donation to the world service organization of its affiliation, its intergroup, or the purchase of its literature.

INTERGROUP

Many locations have a sufficient number of groups to support a central office which will provide an answering service, network new meetings, print a meeting list, and other services. Intergroups are generally supported by contributions and purchases of literature from groups.

A Suggested ACOA Meeting Format

The following meeting format for adult children of alcoholics has evolved over the last several years. This is a mature format which has successfully met the needs of the group. Instructions to the group chairperson are in brackets. My commentary is in *italic* in the left column. Selections to be read out loud are in **boldface**.

1. Opening.
[Read by the chairperson.]

The Serenity Prayer is a nondenominational prayer first written by Reinhold Neibuhr. The second and third verses are rarely used by self-help groups, perhaps because of their implied sectarian content. The prayer was originally adopted by AA in 1942. Its beauty lies in its addressing of the control issues which plague so many of us.

May we please have a moment of silence? to be followed by the Serenity Prayer.

God, grant me the serenity to accept the things I cannot change, Courage to change the things I can, and Wisdom to know the difference.

2. Welcome.
[Read by the chairperson.]

This welcome was borrowed and adapted from a pamphlet issued by the Seattle, Washington Adult Children of Alcoholics Intergroup. Seattle received it from a group in Scottsdale, Arizona, which in turn received it from a group in Westwood, California. The welcome dates from 1980. Some groups may want to use an adaptation of the Alateen Welcome which is eloquent, positive, and hopeful.

We welcome you to this meeting of Adult Children of Alcoholics. Many of us coming to these meetings were distressed and in some stage of unresolved grief. We felt that we had lost or given up so much in our lives that we had nothing more to give. We needed to understand what had happened to us as children. We needed to validate the reality that there was a problem—that it just wasn't our imagination.

We give up nothing except our denial. We need no longer

continue doing what we did as children to survive. We need to free ourselves of the pain of our past. We need to come out of our dreamlike state, dropping layers of denial. We need to lose our extreme need to control. We need to put some order to the many years of seeking answers in books, psychotherapy, self-reliance, and conversations with friends and professionals who don't understand and can't help.

Today, realizing that it was all valuable and part of our growth experience that brought us to this new beginning, we now enter into the process of selfdiscovery. The Twelve Steps of Recovery contain a solution for dealing with the alcoholism of our family of origin and its effect on our character. In this group we work through our stages of grief and feel and express the feelings and emotions that we never allowed ourselves to feel and express in our own families. We do this by sharing "what happened" and "what's happening now" in a safe and loving environment. By re-creating in the present what happened to us as children, we can break the bondage of survival patterns which are holdovers from our traumatic childhoods, deal with unresolved problems in our past, and learn to live full lives.

At this meeting you can expect to get in touch with emotions you have denied until now. It may be fear; it may be anger, it may be unexpressed love; it may be all of these emotions and more. If you have a simple heartfelt desire for happy and effective living, then we hope you will join us as we give freely of what we have found.

3. Hello
[The Chairperson introduces himself/herself. Group members introduce themselves with first names and name of the town they live in. This allows people to network while preserving anonymity.]

Hello. I'm [name] from [town].

4. The Problem and the Solution.
[Have The Problem and The Solution read by a member of the group.]

Although the "Problem and Solution" which follows leans heavily on the "Problem and Solution" which originated in New York City in the late 1970s, it is a completely reworked text. The author (or authors) of this version is unknown. The original "Problem and Solution" was written by Tony A., then of New York City, and now of Florida.[3] Partici-

The Problem:

Many of us found we had several characteristics in common as a result of being brought up in alcoholic households. We had come to feel isolated, uneasy with other people, especially authority figures. To protect ourselves, we became people pleasers, even though we lost our own identities in the process. Personal criticism we perceived as a threat.

We either became alcoholics ourselves or married them—or both. Failing that, we found another compulsive personality

---

3. See A., Tony. (1991). *The laundry list*. Deerfield Beach, FL: Health Communications.

pation of other group members in reading this essay builds self-confidence.

such as a workaholic with whom we could continue the kind of relationships we had with our alcoholic parents.

We lived life from the standpoint of victims. Having an overdeveloped sense of responsibility, we preferred to be concerned with others rather than ourselves. We felt guilty when we stood up for ourselves. We became reactors rather than actors, letting others take the initiative.

We were dependent personalities—terrified of abandonment, willing to do almost anything to hold on to a relationship in order not to be abandoned emotionally. We kept choosing insecure relationships because they matched our childhood relationships with alcoholic parents.

These symptoms of the family disease of alcoholism made us like alcoholics—we took on many of the characteristics of alcoholism without necessarily ever taking a drink. We learned to stuff our feelings as children and kept them buried as adults. We chose not to talk or trust or feel. As a result of our conditioning we confused love with pity, tending to love those we could rescue. Even more self-defeating, we became addicted to excitement, preferring constant upset to workable relationships. This is a description. It is not an indictment.

The Solution:

The solution is to become your own parent, and to join in the process of healing through the Twelve Steps of Recovery one day at a time.

By attending these meetings on a regular basis, you will come to see parental alcoholism for what it is: a disease that infected you as a child and which continues to affect you as an adult. When you let go of the denial, you will learn that the disease of alcoholism caused you to be without the parenting you needed as a child. You will go through the process of grieving. You will learn what healing is and how you can get it for yourself.

You will not have to do this alone. Look around you and you will see others who know exactly how you feel. We know where you're coming from because we've been there ourselves. We will love and support you no matter what. We want you to accept us as brothers and sisters, just as we already accept you.

This is a spiritual program based on honesty, trust, and love. We are sure that as our program of recovery grows inside you, you will see beautiful changes in all of your relationships, especially with your parents, your Higher Power and yourself.

5. The Twelve Steps of Recovery.

[Have the Twelve Steps of Recovery read by a group member.]

When the Twelve Steps of Alcoholics Anonymous, from which these steps were adapted were originally written, Step Twelve anticipated groups for spouses and children of alcoholics by its original language: "Having had a spiritual experience as the result of this course of action, we tried to carry this message to others, especially alcoholics, and to practice these principles in all our affairs."4 It's important to note that these steps are only suggested. Neither AA nor any of its offspring offer the only route to recovery. Nevertheless, the suggestions expressed here have resulted in recoveries of countless thousands of persons.

"Here are the steps we took, which are suggested as a program of recovery.

1. We admitted we were powerless over alcohol—that our lives had become unmanageable.

2. Came to believe that a Power greater than ourselves could restore us to sanity.

3. Made a decision to turn our will and our lives over to the care of God as we understood Him.

4. Made a searching and fearless moral inventory of ourselves.

5. Admitted to God, to ourselves, and to another human being the exact nature of our wrongs.

6. Were entirely ready to have God remove all these defects of character.

7. Humbly asked him to remove our shortcomings.

---

4. See the quotes from the multilith edition of Alcoholics Anonymous, in Pittman, B. (1988). *AA, the way it began*. Seattle: Glen Abbey Books.

8. Made a list of all persons we had harmed, and became willing to make amends to them all.

9. Made direct amends to such people wherever possible, except when to do so would injure them or others.

10. Continued to take personal inventory and when we were wrong promptly admitted it.

11. Sought through prayer and meditation to improve our conscious contact with God as we understood Him, praying only for knowledge of His will for us and the power to carry that out.

12. Having had a spiritual awakening as the result of these Steps, we tried to carry this message to Alcoholics,* and to practice these principles in all our affairs.

6. Daily Meditation

[Have a group member read today's selection from *One Day at a Time in Al-Anon* or *Alateen-A Day at a Time.*[5]]

*Groups may want to substitute the word "others" for "Alcoholics."

5. Al-Anon Family Groups, Inc. (1973). *One day at a time in Al-Anon.* New York: Author and Al-Anon Family Groups, Inc. (1983). *Alateen-a day at a time.* New York: Author.

*Groups may want to substitute
a reading from a daily
meditation book written
especially for adult children
of alcoholics. Reading of any
daily meditation book provides
a centering focus for the day.*

7. Newcomers

[Ask those who are here for
the first, second, or third
meeting to raise their hands.
Welcome them. Suggest that
they try to get to as many
meetings as they can for the
next ninety days. Tell them
where they can get meeting
lists.]

*This is a supportive and
accepting gesture. The
suggestion is made because
some ACOAs may want to be all
better in one meeting. The
therapy of the group is in the
meeting. The more meetings
attended, the more therapy
received.*

8. Old-timers

[Ask the members of the
steering committee to raise
their hands, and tell everyone
that these people, having been
around for a while, are the
people to go and talk to after
the meeting.]

*The steering committee usually
consists of former officers of
the group or those who have
the most self-help group
experience. Since ACOA groups
are sometimes short of*

experienced members, this is a
wise, protective measure.

9. Flashbacks

[Remind the group that
flashbacks happen. If they
remember some pain from their
past, suggest they either make
a note of it or remember it
and talk about it with someone
before they go home. It
doesn't help to stuff it
anymore.]

10. Announcements

[1. Announce the formation and
location of other group
meetings, individual and group
anniversaries, etc.
[2. Note that there is
literature available for those
who want it. Note the terms
at which literature may be
obtained.]

Usually pamphlets are free and
hardcover or book-length
literature is sold at cost and
on terms acceptable to the
group and to the group member.

[3. Note that the group has no
dues or fees, but does have
expenses for literature, rent,
and coffee. Then pass the
basket.]

Passing the basket at this
time insures that it will not
be forgotten or disrupt the
meeting.

11. Small Group Meetings.

ACOA meetings have a tendency to grow very large in a short amount of time. In order to allow everyone to have a chance to speak, it is usually necessary to break into smaller groups if the circumstances of the meeting place permit this. If the group must of necessity stay large, it needs to limit comments by group members to a few minutes if the meeting is to last no more than an hour. Meetings which go on and on and on tend to be antitherapeutic. Keeping members' comments short and to the point keeps any one person from monopolizing or dominating the group.

[Announce the type and location of meetings to be held this evening.]

1. Speaker meeting.
[Introduce the speaker.]

Speaker meetings are generally open to persons who are not Adult Children of Alcoholics. The term "Adult Children of Alcoholics" generally includes those who were raised by a parent or parent figure who was a problem drinker, or who is the grandchild of an alcoholic. Some meetings have one speaker, followed by a discussion period. Others will have more than one speaker. The group chairperson needs to announce whether or not the group is open or closed to outsiders. Here is one vote for making all speaker meetings open meetings.

2. Index meeting.
[Ask for topic]

The subject of this meeting is taken from the "One Day at a Time in Al-Anon" or other daily meditation book suitable for Adult Children of Alcoholics.[6] A day's selection is read to start off the meeting and to focus on the topic. Each person in turn shares their personal feeling or experience.

3. Characteristics of ACOAs meeting.

[Ask for the topic.]

Characteristics can be drawn from the "Problem and Solution," or from any other list the group agrees on.

4. Roles meeting.
[Ask for topic]

Common roles are: Hero, Scapegoat, Lost Child, Mascot/Clown, Enabler, Survivor, Victim, Distancer, Pursuer.

After the small group meetings, we will meet back here for a formal closing, and for discussion, fellowship and coffee.

---

6. Current choices are Lerner, Rokelle. (1985). *Daily affirmations.* Pompano Beach, FL: Health Communications; Larsen, E. (1987). *Days of healing, days of joy.* New York: HarperCollins; Anonymous. (1985). *This new day.* Delaware Water Gap, PA: Quotidian.

5. Keeping Current Meeting.

[For those who have a current
success or problem they can't
keep to themselves any
longer.]

12. Closing

*The closing statement can be
read by either the chairperson
to the group as a whole, or by
the leader of each small
group.*

In closing, remember that
what is said here represents
only the opinion of the person
speaking. Take what you like
and leave the rest.

Remember that ACOA meetings
can teach us to feel, trust,
and talk. We learn to meet our
own needs and to solve our own
problems intelligently.

Prayer and meditation will
give us a better understanding
of ourselves and our
relationship to our Higher
Power and to our fellow human
beings.

Remember not to go home with
brand-new pain. Talk
with someone. Try to work
things through with another
member of the group. Hold
what you have heard here
confidential. There is no
room in our recovery for
gossip or criticism. Allow
the healing of our program of
recovery to nourish you one
day at a time.

Will all who care to, join
me in the closing prayer?

*A universal, nondenominational
prayer such as the Serenity
Prayer is often chosen to
provide closure to the
meeting. Many groups choose*

God grant me the serenity to
accept the things I cannot
change, courage to change
things I can, and wisdom to know
the difference.

*the Lord's Prayer, but this is
often objected to by non-
Christians because of its
Christian origin.*

A final note. I have long believed that much, if not most, of what is therapeutic about self-help groups occurs not at the meeting, which is only a catalyst for growth, but outside in the parking lot, or later at a diner where group members congregate after the meeting.

This is only one format among many. There is no "one" way to do a group. Any format you choose or adapt and which works well for you is the right one.

APPENDIX 2

Intergroup Control Issues

Al-Anon Family Groups, Inc., the World Service Office that represents all autonomous Al-Anon groups, has a unique service structure that many individuals have difficulty in understanding.

Unlike most organizations, Al-Anon is organized from the bottom up, rather than from the top down. Probably the purest of democratic organizations, Al-Anon's World Service Office, by design, does not control or enforce its will on the groups. Rather, it receives its directions from the groups. There are many fringe benefits to this practice. It is very difficult, for example, for a self-help group following Al-Anon's practices, to become a cult. This is an especially acute problem, because so many of Al-Anon's members have unresolved control issues. Al-Anon members in the early stages of recovery may be more likely to manifest overcontrolling behaviors at one extreme, or victim roles at the other.

Thus, many adult children groups within Al-Anon have experienced a hostile reaction from other Al-Anon groups and from Information Service Committees (Intergroups) over the last ten years. The hostile reaction usually takes the form of objections to the adult children's group choice of format or literature, followed by a threat to delist the meeting from the area meeting list. As a result, adult children's groups in many states have chosen to leave Al-Anon because of unwanted interference with their autonomy.

One of the issues that remain unresolved is the question of whether or not adult children's groups within the Al-Anon framework may or should use outside literature or vary their format according to their own will.

My own view is that the self-help movement, especially that of Alcoholics Anonymous, has thrived on heresy and dissent. For example, neither Bill Wilson nor Bob Smith, the cofounders of Alcoholics Anonymous, were initially in favor of any of the following: rotation of group leaders, breaking away from organized religion (i.e., the Oxford Group), newsletters, Alcoholics Anonymous as the name of the organization, cheap paperback editions of the book *Alcoholics Anonymous,* and acceptance of women and Catholics as members of AA. Yet all of these, the product of an AA heretic by the name of Clarence Snyder, were to become integral parts of AA.

The adult children's movement is one that came about because of books. Books are and have been an integral part of this recovery movement quite unlike those of its predecessors. This is partly because there was a tremendous vacuum created by Al-Anon Family Groups, which chose (and wisely, I think) to wait before developing literature of its own for adult children. Al-Anon tries to avoid currently fashionable psychological jargon, believing that their therapy comes mostly from people sharing of experience, strength, and hope with one another.

I agree. Of all the things that are healing in groups, all come from the interaction of one person with another, and not from books. There is a further danger that is very grave to all self-help groups. That is when some person enters a self-help meeting and holds up a book of one authority or another, and states to all that this book or that holds all the answers. It doesn't make any difference whether or not that book is the Bible, or the Big Book of Alcoholics Anonymous. Whenever this happens, the meeting ceases to be a self-help group, and becomes an authority group. No book is more than a tool for recovery, and when it has outlived its usefulness, it is to be discarded in favor of another.

Listen to me. This is Tom Perrin, the bookseller, speaking. If you want to buy books about recovery, go to a bookstore. If you want to recover, go to a self-help group meeting. Don't mix the two up. It's that simple.

Normally, the internal affairs of any one self-help group would not be of any interest to anyone outside the group. However, the interference of self-appointed guardians in the internal affairs of individual self-help groups is such a common problem that it has national consequences, and affects the self-help group movement as a whole. The following text is one Adult Children's Al-Anon Group response to interference in their internal affairs:

> On July 31, 1990, the Information Service Representatives (ISRs) of the North Jersey Al-Anon Groups will be making a very important decision when they meet in Montclair. The North Jersey Information Service Steering Committee proposed a motion for the approval of the ISRs as follows: "If the Information Service receives repeated complaints about any Al-Anon group not conforming to the traditions, will the steering committee be authorized to remove

them from the North Jersey Al-Anon Information Service meeting list?" The steering committee is deciding on a procedure to be followed (if this motion is passed) before an Al-Anon meeting can be removed from the meeting list.

We believe that a procedure for monitoring group conduct by a steering committee, or individuals of that committee, has been and would continue to be very damaging to the spirit of our program of recovery. We believe that the proper way for an Al-Anon member to express his or her concern (not "complaint") about any Al-Anon group not conforming to the traditions would be for that member to speak directly with members of the group in question, personally, in the meeting, or in the business meeting, to reason things out and to resolve the problem internally and democratically. It is not in the spirit of the program to pass on our responsibilities to someone else who would try to enforce "obedience to the unenforceable." In *Al-Anon's Twelve Steps and Twelve Traditions,* on page 86, it states: "The traditions are not rules. There are no rules, no 'musts' in Al-Anon. Accepting the guidelines of the Traditions has been described as 'obedience to the unenforceable.' No one in our fellowship has the authority to say 'You should not do this' or "You must do that.'"

Tradition Two states that "For our group purpose there is but one authority-a loving God as He may express Himself in our group conscience. Our leaders are but trusted servants, they do not govern." Again, in the *Twelve Steps and Twelve Traditions,* on page 95, it states: "The progress of the members can be endangered when someone forgets that there is but 'one authority' and that authority is not an individual member, nor even a clique which considers itself special. No one speaks for God; it is a loving God as He may express himself to each of us who forms our group conscience." Continuing on the same page, it reads: "Using this principle helps the group when an occasional member knows all the answers and tries to control the group or make independent decisions for it. Such a person may be motivated by good intentions, but behind it there is always the thought: 'I know what's best.' When an individual member assumes such authority, he or she prevents the others from participation that is so vital to everyone's growth."

The following information was published in the *1989 Summary Al-Anon World Service Conference* on pages 19 and 34.

"What action should an Information Service Office take if it disapproves of the group's practices or format? The workshop assigned this question felt the Area Information Service is there at the will of the group. They do not grant permission. (Also see *Policy*

Digest, pages 12 and 24)." When asked what to do about a group wanting to "do their own thing," the workshop suggested the following: "Provide them with as much information possible about the benefits of adhering to the Traditions...After we have provided information in a loving manner, we can "Let Go and Let God"..."Our Service Concepts remind us that no punitive action should be taken. The purpose of an Al-Anon Information Service Office is to represent and serve groups. No service arm "polices" the group it serves. Nowhere in the Constitution of the North Jersey Information Service is there any mention of the intention to monitor the practices of the meetings it was created to serve.

In *Al-Anon's Twelve Concepts of Service*, under Warranty Five, (Page 43) it points out the "extraordinary liberties which the traditions accord to the individual member and group. No penalties are to be inflicted for non-conformity to Al-Anon principals."

Furthermore, in *Digest of Al-Anon and Alateen Policies*, page 11 under Autonomy of Groups, it states: "It is not within the authority of Al-Anon Information Services to close a group because they disapprove of the manner in which a group practices the Al-Anon program." We believe that in that spirit, it also would not be within the authority of the Information Service to delete a group from the meeting list. "The will of the group determined their scope of function."

Not informing the public about Al-Anon groups that exist is an obvious interference with Step Twelve—"Having had a spiritual awakening as the result of these steps, we tried to carry this message to others and to practice these principles in all our affairs." Misinforming the public is certainly not the proper function of an Information Service. Delisting a group is not about harmony and unity. It is institutional willfulness and divisive.

Al-Anon Family Group Headquarters has never delisted a meeting against the will of that meeting. We think the information service should follow that example. The founders of Al-Anon believed that an unhealthy meeting would die of its own accord. The healing of a group must come from its own conscience.

Our Al-Anon meeting was recently delisted by the information service Steering Committee against our wishes. That mistake was corrected when we were relisted by a vote of the Information Service Representatives (ISRs) in April. Our understanding of the Steps, Traditions, Concepts, and Policies of Al-Anon indicates this motion to allow Information Service to delist a group against its wishes should not even be open to a vote. Unfortunately, it is scheduled to be voted on at the next ISR meeting. Our ISR is going to vote against this motion. We feel very strongly that for the good of our beloved program, this motion should not pass. Since strong opinions and feelings exist on all sides of this issue, it is vitally important that either your group's ISR or Group Representative (GR) be present to vote on this motion at the next quarterly ISR meeting. If your group has no ISR or GR, please decide on a member of your group to be your ISR or GR and represent your group's conscience on this motion. It is important that each group send a representative to this meeting.

Please be there to represent your feelings about this issue. The spirit of responsibility in Al-Anon is at stake. We plead with you to have faith in the Serenity, Courage, and Wisdom of the Program.

God grant me the Serenity
To accept the things I cannot change,
Courage to change the things I can,
And Wisdom to Know the difference.

Stirling Friday Night
Al-Anon Adult Children Group

On July 31, 1990, the resolution to delist meetings, which was opposed by the Stirling Group, was voted down by a narrow margin. A subsequent attempt to delist meetings was made by the Intergroup steering committee by altering the resolution slightly. This second attempt was also voted down by approximately the same margin as before.

The arguments made by the Stirling, NJ group are persuasive, healthy, and in accordance with the Twelve Traditions of Al-Anon Family Groups. If your group has problems similar to the ones outlined here, you might want to take a long look at what the Stirling group has done to exercise its autonomy and follow their successful example.

Acknowledgments

Any author publishing a book for the first time is beholden to such a pantheon of greater mortals that to list all the persons who have influenced him and the development of his thought and writing might occupy the major portion of the book.

Thus, if I have left anyone unmentioned who should have been mentioned, it is for reasons of space, rather than for reasons of intentional neglect. I could not be the person I am were it not for the influence of my surrogate parents, Pal and Bob Port, Bill and Marie Cole, Charlotte and Doyle Jones, and the priests and brothers of College Bourget, Rigaud, Quebec. I am sure that their unconditional love saved the emotional lives of many others in addition to myself. Donald Parisian and Kelsie Harder were the very best of teachers, each reaching me in ways that transcended their disciplines. The lessons in group process that I learned from Mary Ruzicka, Tony Palisi, and Henry Schreitmueller have stood up for over ten years; I expect them to last a lifetime. Janet Woititz was the right person, in the right place, at the right time. She was the first to validate the idea that my ignorance of socially appropriate coping skills was neither willful nor pathological and to understand that my behaviors, now maladaptive, were necessary to my survival in childhood. Her knowledge of children of alcoholics, and her voice of passion helped change the course of psychological history. She also brought together in one place Sue Nobleman, Debbie, Rob, and myself, to each of whom I shall forever be grateful. Sharon Cruse in her book *Another Chance, Hope and Health for the Alcoholic Family* provided a framework of alcoholic family roles which has withstood the test of time. Sharon and Joe's workshops in South Dakota were important elements in my recov-

163

ery, which I could never have experienced had it not been for their friendship and support. Charles Deutsch wrote the first book about children of alcoholics I ever sold. The scholarship and eloquence of *Broken Bottles, Broken Dreams* provide us with the standard by which this and all other books on children of alcoholics are to be measured. Carolyn Kleinman was my first partner in the treatment of survivors of incest and familial alcoholism. Her support and expertise were essential ingredients in the recovery of many, including myself. I am awed by my therapy clients. Much of what I know about myself came about because of their willingness to trust and share their lives, their feelings, and their minds. I confess to being somewhat mystified by Mike Leach and Gene Gollogly, my principals at Crossroad/Continuum, who seem to understand what I am trying to do with my life without my having to explain it. Mary-Lynne Vanderbilt Pfeiffer, who has known me in good times and bad since we were children together, graciously loaned me the peace and privacy of her home in the Adirondacks where the core of this book was written. Without her assistance, I would have always found something else to do. None of this book could have happened without my parents, who for decades fought a disease they didn't know they had. Growing up in their alcoholic family is a little bit like being in the army. I don't think I would volunteer for it a second time, but I'm grateful for the experience and would not trade it or them for any other. Their sobriety proves that our lives would have been very different had they not been afflicted by this disease. No persons have brought me more joy and happiness than my wife Janice Treggett and our son Charles Treggett Perrin. Janice's support and encouragement directly contributed to words being put on paper rather than written on air. More importantly, I am grateful that Janice has found the courage and strength to live with a truly difficult author-person. Charlie's consistent good humor provides promise that the cycle of depressive spectrum disease and family dysfunction can be weakened, if not broken.

Copyright Acknowledgments

About the Author

Thomas W. Perrin is an alcoholism counselor in private practice with a masters degree in alcoholism and group process from Seton Hall University. He has been conducting groups and workshops for adult children of alcoholics since 1981. With his wife Janice Treggett, he also manages Perrin & Treggett Booksellers in East Rutherford and Rocky Hill New Jersey. Perrin & Treggett Booksellers has been a pioneer in the addictions field since 1982 when the Perrins first brought books about children of alcoholics to the attention of the professional community. Their customers and clients now range from Fortune 500 companies to mental health centers, from major television talk shows to schools, municipalities, and the federal government. In 1982, Tom Perrin first published *COA REVIEW, The Newsletter about Children of Alcoholics* from which some of the material in this book has been taken. He lives with his wife and child in New Jersey.